Nicola Frost is a specialist family law barrister at 3PB Barristers. She advises and represents clients in all areas of family finance, including disputes between cohabitants, division of assets upon divorce or dissolution and financial arrangements for children. Nicola has a particular interest and specialist expertise in the area of pre-nuptial and post-nuptial agreements. She is recommended in the Legal 500 as a leading junior barrister in divorce and financial remedy cases. She has been described by judges as 'tenacious' and her written work is often commended. Clients appreciate Nicola's 'no stone unturned' approach to cases and for dealing with them with sensitivity and compassion.

A Practical Guide to Pre-Nuptial and Post-Nuptial Agreements

A Practical Guide to Pre-Nuptial and Post-Nuptial Agreements

Nicola Frost
Barrister, Inner Temple
LL.B (Hons)

Law Brief Publishing

Published 2021 by Law Brief Publishing, an imprint of Law Brief Publishing Ltd
30 The Parks
Minehead
Somerset
TA24 8BT

www.lawbriefpublishing.com

Paperback: 978-1-913715-17-5

Thank you…

To Rachael:

For inspiring me, mentoring me and our true friendship.

To Rob:

For the vision and ideas.

To my parents:

For your encouragement and for being proud.

To my husband and children:

For always being my champions and celebrating with me.

This is all for you.

PREFACE

Nuptial agreements: are they unromantic or proof that a couple is marrying for love and not money? Either way, since the Supreme Court's landmark decision in 2010, pre-nuptial (and post-nuptial) agreements have become more commonplace.

With a high percentage of marriages and civil partnerships coming to an end for a variety of reasons which are usually unforeseeable, consideration of a pre-nuptial agreement probably ought to be a part of wedding preparation, alongside wills (and wedding cake). Whilst there will be common threads of information contained within every nuptial agreement, each should be an entirely bespoke document created for the circumstances of the parties entering it. Parties' intentions regarding their finances should be clearly discussed, set out and recorded in an agreement.

I wanted to write a book that draws in practical tips and suggestions for those advising in respect of nuptial agreements at all stages, from initial consultation, to drafting and upon separation. This book also covers the evolution of nuptial agreements, through the development of case law, and sets out how the court might approach a financial remedies case, with and without the presence of a nuptial agreement. It is written in such a way that the reader can choose to read the book from cover-to-cover or, instead, use it as a reference point when faced with a particular issue.

This book is aimed at family law practitioners dealing with cases involving a nuptial agreement. It may also be useful for an individual considering entering a nuptial agreement or who may have already entered an agreement, whether they are seeking to rely or renege upon it.

Many thanks for your interest in this book – I hope you will find it useful.

The law is up-to-date to 31 July 2021.

Nicola Frost, Barrister

October 2021

CONTENTS

CASE DIGEST

CHAPTER ONE

NUPTIAL AGREEMENTS

This chapter aims to provide an overview as to what is meant by the term 'nuptial agreement', the development of such agreements and the circumstances which may lead a couple to create one.

What is a Nuptial Agreement?

The term 'nuptial agreement' is used in relation to agreements made between parties to a marriage or civil partnership. It covers pre-nuptial (or ante-nuptial) agreements made prior to marriage, post-nuptial agreements made during marriage, and their civil partnership counterparts: pre-registration agreements and post-registration agreements.[1] They are sometimes referred to as 'marital' agreements or contracts; this term would also encompass separation agreements.

Whilst separation agreements do appear in the development of case law relating to nuptial agreements,[2] they are quite a different form of marital agreement because the parties have already separated and the terms of the agreement are based on contemporaneous circumstances. Pre-nuptial and post-nuptial agreements, which this book focuses upon, are agreements entered into contingent upon a future set of circumstances which may have changed by the time the agreement comes to be relied upon.

Nuptial agreements commonly set out which party owns – or will own – certain capital assets and how they will be dealt with in the event of a

---

[1] Throughout this book, references to pre-nuptial agreements or post-nuptial agreements should be taken to encompass pre-registration agreements and post-registration agreements, respectively.

[2] For example, see *Edgar v Edgar* [1980] EWCA Civ 2

future breakdown of the marriage or civil partnership. It is usual for an agreement to define 'matrimonial', or 'joint', property and 'non-matrimonial', or 'separate', property.

Matrimonial (or joint) property usually includes assets held in joint names and non-matrimonial (or separate) property normally comprises pre-owned or pre-acquired assets, inherited assets and gifts received during the marriage or civil partnership. A nuptial agreement should ringfence only surplus, separate, property and those drafting should always ensure that both parties' needs are met.

A nuptial agreement may also include reference to income, insofar as how earnings, future earnings and interests under trusts will be dealt with during and at the conclusion of a marriage or civil partnership. However, it should be noted that a nuptial agreement cannot purport to exclude periodical payments; to do so would put the entire agreement at risk.[3]

It is not uncommon for a pre-nuptial agreement to be updated, perhaps when a change in circumstances arises, and made into a post-nuptial agreement, although it is also possible to create a post-nuptial agreement afresh within a marriage without first having a pre-nuptial agreement.

As the law currently stands, a nuptial agreement is not binding in the jurisdiction of England and Wales, but it is certainly persuasive and could well be determinative. Since the Supreme Court's landmark ruling in ***Radmacher v Granatino***,[4] over a decade ago, it is more likely that a nuptial agreement will be upheld, providing it is 'fair'; however, it will remain subject to the court's discretionary exercise.[5]

---

[3] *Hyman v Hyman* [1929] AC 601; *Z v Z (Financial Remedy: Marriage Contract)* [2011] EWHC 2878

[4] *Radmacher (formerly Granatino) v Granatino* [2010] UKSC 42

[5] Considered further in Chapter 2

Evolution of Nuptial Agreements

Pre-nuptial agreements were initially introduced to the jurisdiction of England and Wales in order to protect the property of women of wealthy families from their husbands, usually by placing their family property upon trust. Prior to the Married Women's Property Act of 1882, the law was that any property owned or brought into the marriage by the wife became her husband's property; indeed, the wife herself became the property of her husband.

As the law in respect of matrimonial finance has developed, notably with the seminal case of ***White v White***,[6] there has been a shift in the approach taken by the courts when apportioning the assets of the parties to a divorce. The contributions of both parties to a marriage, whether financial or practical (i.e. caring for the family and home), are viewed as equivalent to one another. The starting point is therefore equality of division, as between the parties.[7] This also applies in respect of the dissolution of a civil partnership.

Lady Hale, in her dissenting judgment in *Radmacher*,[8] clearly considered a gender dimension to have evolved in respect of pre-nuptial agreements. Lady Hale considered nuptial agreements were created – almost exclusively – to protect a wealthier soon-to-be husband's property from their soon-to-be wife, as an unintended consequence of establishing a foundation of equality upon divorce. It may be seen as an interesting twist of fate that the leading Supreme Court authority on nuptial agreements[9], in which the gender issue was highlighted, actually involved a very wealthy wife and the balance of financial power laid with her.

Today, the picture in respect of the purported gender imbalance is likely reduced by the introduction of civil partnerships (in 2005) and same-sex

---

[6] *White v White* [2000] UKHL 54

[7] See Chapter 2

[8] *Radmacher v Granatino, supra*

[9] *Radmacher v Granatino, supra*

marriage (in 2014). It is, though, unlikely to be evidenced for some years. It has been surmised that the imbalance may not only be financial; there could be emotional inequality[10], which may be more difficult to identify and prove.

Where inequity exists between the parties to an agreement, whether financial or emotional (and sometimes neither will be present), any purported disparity in status is either diminished or negated if both parties freely choose to enter an agreement, have a full appreciation of the terms and implications and have had the benefit of (or at least the opportunity to obtain) independent legal advice. The Supreme Court made it very clear that individuals' autonomous choice to deal with their finances as set out in their agreement ought to be respected, although the court retains its overall discretion so as to ensure that any financial settlement on divorce or dissolution is fair.

The court must approve *all* financial orders on divorce or dissolution, whether a consent order has been filed for the court's approval (with no court hearings) or if the parties have required the assistance of the court to decide how their assets should be divided between them. The court will carry out its discretionary exercise taking into account all the circumstances of the case. As practitioners will be aware, it is simply not possible to oust the jurisdiction of the court.

Reasons for Creating an Agreement

A nuptial agreement is a way of setting out the parties' financial intentions at the outset of, or within, a marriage or civil partnership in order to define joint and separate property. Some consider nuptial agreements to be unromantic, but they allow individuals to command their independence and create a mutual understanding of how they intend to deal with their finances. They perhaps ought to be viewed, alongside wills and wedding cake, as an essential part of wedding

---

[10] *B v S (Financial Remedy: Marital Property Regime)* [2012] EWHC 265

planning. It has even been suggested (by Katrin Radmacher) that the existence of a pre-nuptial agreement would be proof that the parties married for love and not for money.[11]

As a nuptial agreement is neither contractually binding nor automatically upheld by a court, it remains to be considered as one of the circumstances of the case[12] or conduct it would be inequitable to disregard.[13] Given its lack of contractual force, some wonder whether it is worth going to the time and expense of creating a nuptial agreement; however, post *Radmacher*, it is likely that an agreement that is well drafted, well considered and – above all – 'fair' will be upheld. However, what is 'fair' is subjective and may change over time.

Nuptial agreements may be used in order to protect assets owned prior to marriage and are particularly beneficial where:

- there are children from a previous marriage (to ringfence pre-acquired assets for the benefit of these children and general inheritance planning);
- there are business assets;
- there are family trusts or properties;
- there are future inheritance prospects[14] or inherited assets;
- either party has a connection with another jurisdiction;
- one party has a substantially greater asset base or income than the other;

---

[11] *Radmacher v Granatino, supra,* at [13]

[12] *Brack v Brack* [2018] EWCA Civ 2862; *KA v MA (Pre-Nuptial Agreement – Needs)* [2018] EWHC 499; *K v K (Ancillary Relief: Pre-Nuptial Agreement)* [2003] 1 FLR 120; *M v M (Pre-Nuptial Agreement)* [2002] 1 FLR 654

[13] *Hyman v Hyman* [1929] AC 601; *M v M (Pre-Nuptial Agreement)* [2002] 1 FLR 654; *Luckwell v Limata* [2014] EWHC 502

[14] Note that advice on wills may be required

- both parties have pre-acquired wealth or assets;
- either party has been married before.

Whilst, since *Radmacher*, individual autonomy is now considered to be of elevated importance, nuptial agreements are often prepared many years in advance of the time upon which they come to be relied. Review clauses are not always adhered to and circumstances can – and often do – change. If the court did not retain its final authority, there is a risk that one party could be left in a predicament of real need. A tempered individual autonomy is therefore likely to continue.

Whilst it may be unlikely that anyone entering a marriage intends to rely upon the terms of a pre-nuptial agreement, its existence does not mean that divorce is inevitable. What it does mean is that, in the unfortunate event of a breakdown of the marriage or civil partnership, the parties' recorded intentions may be used as a basis for drafting a consent order. Generally, parties entering an agreement have the ultimate aim of limiting post-separation litigation which can otherwise often result in great financial and emotional cost and uncertainty.

CHAPTER TWO

THE COURT'S DISCRETIONARY EXERCISE

This Chapter contains an overview of the applicable law in financial remedy cases. There is consideration of the court's statutory discretionary exercise, the applicable principles and the way in which non-matrimonial property is usually treated.

The Statutory Criteria[1]

A discretionary jurisdiction exists in financial remedy cases. The court has the power to make various orders within financial proceedings following the breakdown of a marriage or civil partnership. The court's power is derived from section 25 of the Matrimonial Causes Act 1973 for divorcing couples and Schedule 5, Part 5 of the Civil Partnership Act 2004 for those dissolving their civil partnership.

The statutory provisions enable the court to make orders for periodical payments (spousal maintenance) or lump sum orders[2], property adjustment orders (transfers of property)[3], orders for the sale of property[4] and pension sharing orders.[5] The court must make an order that is fair in all the circumstances of the case[6], having regard to a number of factors

[1] 'Section 25 Criteria' under the Matrimonial Causes Act 1973 ('MCA') and 'Schedule 5 Criteria' in respect of the Civil Partnership Act 2004 ('CPA')

[2] Section 23, MCA 1973

[3] Section 24, MCA 1973

[4] Section 24A, MCA 1973

[5] Section 24B, MCA 1973; section 24E, MCA 1973

[6] Section 25(1), MCA 1973

that are listed in section 25(2) of the Matrimonial Causes Act 1973 and Schedule 5, Part 5 of the Civil Partnership Act 2004. Whichever order(s) the court makes, it must have first regard to any minor child or children of the family.[7]

As the court's first consideration, children ought not to be prejudiced by any orders made by the court. Often, the court will be tasked with ensuring the housing needs of the children of the family (and their primary carer) are met.

In making its decision, the court must have regard to the statutory criteria set down in section 25 of the Matrimonial Causes Act 1973, commonly known as 'the section 25 criteria', or 'the section 25 factors':

> "(1) It shall be the duty of the court in deciding whether to exercise its powers... and, if so, in what manner, to have regard to all the circumstances of the case, first consideration being given to the welfare while a minor of any child of the family who has not attained the age of eighteen.
>
> (2) As regards the exercise of the powers of the court... in relation to a party to the marriage, the court shall in particular have regard to the following matters—
>
> (a) the income, earning capacity, property and other financial resources which each of the parties to the marriage has or is likely to have in the foreseeable future, including in the case of earning capacity any increase in that capacity which it would in the opinion of the court be reasonable to expect a party to the marriage to take steps to acquire;
>
> (b) the financial needs, obligations and responsibilities which each of the parties to the marriage has or is likely to have in the foreseeable future;
>
> (c) the standard of living enjoyed by the family before the breakdown of the marriage;

[7] Section 25(1), MCA 1973

(d) the age of each party to the marriage and the duration of the marriage;

(e) any physical or mental disability of either of the parties to the marriage;

(f) the contributions which each of the parties has made or is likely in the foreseeable future to make to the welfare of the family, including any contribution by looking after the home or caring for the family;

(g) the conduct of each of the parties, if that conduct is such that it would in the opinion of the court be inequitable to disregard it;

(h) in the case of proceedings for divorce or nullity of marriage, the value to each of the parties to the marriage of any benefit . . . which, by reason of the dissolution or annulment of the marriage, that party will lose the chance of acquiring."[8]

The section 25 criteria are mirrored in the Civil Partnership Act 2004.[9] It was stated in ***Lawrence v Gallagher* [2012] EWCA Civ 394** that the fact that a claim arises from the dissolution of a civil partnership rather than on divorce is of little significance. Throughout this book, references to the section 25 criteria should be taken to also include the mirrored criteria as set out in Schedule 5, Part 5 of the Civil Partnership Act 2004.

In every case, the application of the section 25 factors will differ. There is no hierarchy in respect of the factors.[10] Some elements will be attributed more weight than others and, in many cases, one factor will stand out and will be the 'magnetic' factor.[11] Each case will be entirely fact-specific.

It is key to note that the application of the section 25 principles, and having regard to all the circumstances of the case, is a discretionary

---

[8] Section 25, MCA 1973

[9] Civil Partnership Act 2004, Sch. 5, Part 5

[10] *Piglowska v Piglowski* [1999] 1 WLR 1360

[11] *Gordon (formerly Stefanou) v Stefanou* [2010] EWCA Civ 1601

exercise for the judge. This means that there is a range of reasonableness and, on a given day, different judges faced with the same facts may attribute varying weight to the same section 25 factors to come to a range of decisions. That is not to say that any of those judges would be wrong, but the result could be quite different. The outcome cannot, therefore, be guaranteed.

The starting point in any financial remedies case is equality[12] but the various section 25 factors may be applied so as to lead to a departure from equality. The three principles of 'needs', 'sharing' and 'compensation' will apply; however, in all financial provision cases, the 'needs' principle will always prevail. The court has a duty to consider a clean break in every case[13], although this is not always possible or, indeed, fair.

In all financial remedies cases, there are two stages to the court's decision: the first is the computation stage, where the values of the parties' assets are ascertained, and the distribution stage, where the split of assets is determined.[14] This may require consideration as to which assets are or are not matrimonial in nature, and there may be arguments as to what constitutes matrimonial property.

Fairness: Needs, Compensation and Sharing

The House of Lords made it clear, in ***White v White*** **[2000] UKHL 54**, that fairness is the guiding principle in financial remedy proceedings and that the court's section 25 discretionary exercise should be checked against the "yardstick of equality of division".[15] The court emphasised the equality of contributions made by both parties to a marriage, whether financial or practical care of the family and home, and cautioned that equality should be departed from only if there was good reason to do so.

---

12 *White v White* [2000] UKHL 54

13 Section 25A, MCA 1973

14 *Holt v Holley & Steer Solicitors* [2020] EWCA Civ 851

15 *White v White, supra, per* Lord Nicholls at [25]

Prior to *White*, there had been a distinction drawn between the breadwinner and the homemaker and claims had been limited to 'reasonable needs' (often resulting in lengthy and costly litigation arguing over what constituted those reasonable needs).

Although a caveat was given, in *White*, that the decision did not intend to introduce a legal presumption of a true 50/50 starting point (it being said that to do so would be an "...impermissible judicial gloss on the statutory provision..."[16]), in practice, the impact of this seminal case was to do just that. The Court of Appeal later confirmed, in ***Charman v Charman*** **[2007] EWCA Civ 503**, that the parties' financial contributions and those in respect of the welfare of the family should generally lead to an equal division of the assets, unless there is a good reason to depart from equality. It is undoubtedly well-established that contributions to the upbringing of the family, whether monetary or practical, are viewed as equal in law.

The overarching principle in any financial remedies case is always to ensure that the outcome is 'fair', but there may well be a divergence of opinion as to what is fair, often based on the parties' subjective perceptions of fairness. As stated by Lord Nicholls of Birkenhead in *White v White*:

> "...the outcome ought to be as fair as is possible in all the circumstances. But everyone's life is different. Features which are important when assessing fairness differ in each case. And, sometimes, different minds can reach different conclusions on what fairness requires. ...**fairness, like beauty, lies in the eye of the beholder.**" [17]

Nonetheless, the court must make an order that it considers to be fair in the circumstances of the case it is faced with.

---

[16] *White v White, supra,* at [27]

[17] *White v White, supra, per* Lord Nicholls of Birkenhead at [1] *(emphasis added)*

The House of Lords helpfully went on to define 'fairness' in the joined appeals of ***Miller v Miller and McFarlane v McFarlane*** **[2006] UKHL 24**. It was stated that there are three principles of fairness which might guide the court in making its award: "…need (generously interpreted), compensation and sharing… The ultimate objective is to give each party an equal start on the road to independent living."[18]

It is possible to alter what might otherwise ultimately have been deemed fair, by entering into a pre-nuptial or post-nuptial agreement.

Needs

The needs of the parties are given priority above any of the other principles and in some cases, there are simply not enough assets to do anything other than to distribute them so as to meet the parties' needs. What constitutes 'needs' will often be fact-specific and therefore differ in every case.

The needs principle encompasses the parties' respective need for a home, their income needs and their needs in retirement. The court will strive to achieve a fair result that meets needs; the compensation and sharing principles are of limited importance in needs-based cases. The parties' standard of living during the marriage or civil partnership will be relevant when the court is assessing 'needs'.

Housing needs

Where there are children, the court should endeavour to stretch the assets, where possible, to ensure that both parents have a home of their own where the children can stay[19]; however, the court does not need to ensure both parties are homeowners[20], and this is particularly so in a

---

[18] *Miller; McFarlane* [2006] UKHL 24, *per* Lady Hale (then Baroness) at [144]

[19] *M v B (lump sum)* [1998] 1 FLR 53, CA

[20] *Cordle v Cordle* [2001] EWCA Civ 1791

needs case. The court can make a variety of orders in relation to property, including transfers, orders for sale or trusts of land; the court can also stipulate that a property is subject to a charge in favour of one of the parties.

Income needs

Although the court will endeavour to achieve a clean break[21], it may be necessary for an order for spousal maintenance to be made, pursuant to section 23 of the Matrimonial Causes Act 1973. This may be made for a specific term, to enable the receiving party to transition to independence, or for the receiving party's lifetime (although joint lives orders are rarely made these days). The periodical payments could remain at a fixed sum or could decrease, again to facilitate the receiving party to achieving independence. It is open to the court to make a nominal spousal maintenance order, which would act simply as a protective measure for the receiving party, in case there were to be a change in circumstances such that he or she would need to apply to vary the order so that it becomes a substantive spousal maintenance order.

Child maintenance is separate to spousal maintenance and a child maintenance liability (contingent upon the family's child arrangements) will arise in every case where there are children, whether via the Child Maintenance Service (CMS), or equivalent body, or ordered by the court. It is important to note that the court has very limited jurisdiction to order child maintenance since the Child Support Act 1991 came into force. Some instances where the court will have jurisdiction include where the paying party earns more than £156,000 gross per annum, where the paying party or the child lives abroad, where the child is no longer a qualifying child for the purposes of the Child Support Act, or where the child is a step-child. It is not possible to circumvent the jurisdiction of the CMS. However, the court is able to make a child maintenance order, by consent, which remains in force until an application is made to the CMS (which either party may do after a period of 12 months).

---

[21] Section 25A, MCA 1973

A court may make a global order for maintenance (often called a 'Segal' order[22]), which is an order covering both spousal and child maintenance. A global order requires that a substantial element must be for spousal maintenance (i.e. it cannot be made where the spousal element is only nominal).[23] The periodical payments are then reduced *pro tanto* by any later child maintenance assessment. The benefit of a global order is that the judge can quantify the level of periodical payments before the Child Maintenance Service have completed its assessment of liability.

Roberts J confirmed the court has jurisdiction to make global orders, in the case of ***AB v CD (Global Maintenance Orders)*** **[2017] EWHC 3164**. However, in *W v H*[24], the court considered that a disaggregated order is often likely to be the better approach if it can be fairly achieved, as a change in circumstances might cause the parties difficulty in the future.[25]

Retirement needs

It is clear from the case of ***W v H*** **[2020] EWFC B10**, that the parties' retirement needs should not be ignored in the search for a fair outcome. The judge, His Honour Judge Hess, was the co-chair of the July 2019 report of the Pension Advisory Group (PAG)[26], which published "...formal guidance to be applied when any issue regarding a pension falls to be determined in financial remedy proceedings..."[27]. The PAG report was quoted with approval throughout the judgment.

It was stated by HHJ Hess that equality of pension income is likely to be the fairest outcome in a financial remedies case and that parties should avoid offsetting pension assets as against other classes of assets, if possible.

---

[22] Named after District Judge Segal, in the Principal Registry

[23] *Dorney-Kingdom v Dorney-Kingdom* [2000] 2 FLR 855

[24] *W v H* [2020] EWFC B10 (considered further below)

[25] *W v H, supra*, at [70]

[26] Pension Advisory Group Report, July 2019: A Guide to the Treatment of Pensions on Divorce

[27] PAG Report, *per* Sir Andrew McFarlane, President of the Family Division

The case also considered whether or not pre-marital contributions and/or accruals should be viewed as non-matrimonial property and therefore whether it would be possible to ringfence them. It was held that, in general, the longer the marriage, the less likely it is that pension accrued outside of the marriage will be ringfenced. The court also held that the pension of £2.1 million firmly kept the case within the confines of a 'needs' case and this was another reason why the pre-marriage accruals were not ringfenced.

Sharing

In cases where the assets exceed the parties' needs (notably in 'big money' cases), the sharing principle will apply to all matrimonial property.

Based on the speech of Lord Nicholls, in *White,* so as to avoid discrimination between the homemaker and the breadwinner, the starting point will be equality, but the court's discretionary application of the section 25 factors may displace this if there is a good reason for doing so.[28] Each element of the statutory criteria will carry varying weight, depending on the facts of the instant case; 'needs' always prevails but other factors, including special contributions and the conduct of the parties may have a bearing on what award the court makes.

Any marital agreement, whether pre-nuptial, post-nuptial or separation, in which the parties state an intention to circumvent the sharing principle will also be considered as one of the circumstances of the case or conduct it would be inequitable to disregard. The existence of a valid nuptial agreement may well be decisive, but caution should be exercised. The sharing principle may not be completely eliminated in all cases; the quest for fairness may – albeit unusually – require a court to make an award in excess of needs.[29]

---

[28] *White v White, supra,* per Lord Nicholls at [25]

[29] *Brack v Brack* [2018] EWCA Civ 2862, *per* Black LJ at [103]

The family home is, distinctive to other property, largely regarded as matrimonial property, regardless of legal title or origin of ownership.[30] The family home will, therefore, invariably be subject to the sharing principle and the starting point will be an equal division of the net equity. Naturally, the application of the needs principle may dictate a departure from equality and an unequal split may also be appropriate where there has been a "...very significant unmatched contribution..." from one party.[31]

As confirmed in the case of ***Sharp v Sharp* [2017] EWCA Civ 408**[32], the sharing principle will generally apply to assets generated within the marriage in all but the rarest of cases. Fairness will usually demand a departure from an equal division of such property following a short, childless, dual career relationship, where finances have been kept separate.[33] The court made it clear, however, that such separation of finances would not be limited solely to those cases where pre-nuptial agreements have been made.[34] Nonetheless, it must be emphasised that, in *Sharp*, the fact the parties had kept their finances completely separate throughout the marriage was just one factor that weighed in the court's discretionary exercise. The original source of property will be more relevant in a short marriage and thus will attract more weight.[35] Another feature which will have a bearing on the distribution of assets as between the parties is the degree to which assets have been mixed, albeit the simple fact of non-matrimonial property having generated an income that has been utilised for the benefit of the family does not automatically classify the asset as matrimonial.[36]

---

30 *Miller; McFarlane* per Lord Nicholls [2006] UKHL 24

31 *FB v PS* [2015] EWHC 2797

32 *Sharp v Sharp* [2017] EWCA Civ 408, *per McFarlane J*

33 *Miller; McFarlane, supra*

34 *Sharp v Sharp, supra, per* McFarlane LJ at [109] and *per* McCombe LJ at [125]

35 *HC v FW* [2017] EWHC 3162

36 *JL v SL (No 2)* [2015] EWHC 360

A broad-brush approach, rather than mathematical precision, is likely to be the most appropriate way to deal with the division of substantial assets, since the intention is to achieve overarching fairness[37], which has a 'broad horizon'.[38] As confirmed by the Court of Appeal in ***Versteegh v Versteegh* [2018] EWCA Civ 1050**, where there is difficulty attributing a value to an asset (in *Versteegh* it was shares held in trust) the fairest approach is likely to be to share it in its present form, such as by making a *Wells* order (as was the court's approach in *Versteegh*).[39]

The treatment of post-separation accumulated wealth (accrued between separation and trial) may[40] or may not[41] be included in the court's application of the sharing principle, although it is settled that future earnings or earning capacity will not be subject to sharing.[42] There is generally no entitlement to future resources.[43]

Compensation

The compensation principle was stated to encompass the final tenet of 'fairness'.[44] It is "...aimed at redressing any significant prospective economic disparity between the parties arising from the way they conducted their marriage..."[45] and, specifically, at circumstances where "...the economic disadvantage generated by the relationship may go beyond need, however generously interpreted..."[46] Lady Hale (then

---

37 *Hart v Hart* [2017] EWCA Civ 1306

38 *Hart v Hart*, supra, *per* Moylan LJ, quoting Lord Nicholls in *Miller*

39 *Wells v Wells* [2002] EWCA Civ 476

40 *B v B* [2013] EWHC 1232 (Fam)

41 *C v C* [2018] EWHC 3186 (Fam)

42 *Waggott v Waggott* [2018] EWCA Civ 727

43 *Miller; McFarlane, supra*

44 *Miller; McFarlane, supra*

45 *Miller, per* Lord Nicholls at [13]

46 *Miller; McFarlane per* Lady Hale at [140]

Baroness) provided a 'best example' for a compensation award: a party having sacrificed – for the benefit of the family – a career that was likely to have been "...lucrative and successful...", along with a high earning spouse who had benefitted from the choices made, and the presence of assets that amount to "...a substantial surplus over what is required to meet both parties' needs..."[47]

As stated by Moylan LJ, in the Court of Appeal in ***Waggott v Waggott*** **[2018] EWCA Civ 727**:

> "...it is clear from *Miller* that compensation is for the "disadvantage" sustained by the party who has given up a career... In practice it is a claim which appears very rarely to have been established and I do not intend to encourage any more extensive or expensive exploration of the issue. However, as a necessary factual foundation the court would have to determine, on a balance of probabilities, that the applicant's career would have resulted in them having resources greater than those which they will be awarded by application of either the need principle or the sharing principle. Further, the court must separately determine whether, and if so how, this factor should be reflected in the award so as to ensure that it is fair to both parties."[48]

A compensation claim is not precluded because the party who chose to give up the career was keen to do so[49] but to the decision must be made for the benefit of the family.[50] Where an award for spousal maintenance is made with a compensation element, the court's assessment of compensation is not limited solely to the end of the marriage but may be

[47] *Miller; McFarlane per* Lady Hale at [140]

[48] *Waggott v Waggott, supra*, at [139]

[49] *Miller; McFarlane* [2006] UKHL 24

[50] *Radmacher (formerly Granatino) v Granatino* [2010] UKSC 42

considered afresh at any subsequent application to vary such a periodical payments order.[51]

In *SA v PA (Pre-Marital Agreement: Compensation)* [2014] **EWHC 392**, Mostyn J, considered the compensation principle:

> (i) would be invoked "...only... in a very rare and exceptional case..."; (ii) where the court could say with "...almost near certainty..." that the party claiming an element of compensation had sacrificed a "...very high earning career which... would have led to earnings at least equivalent to that presently enjoyed by the [other party]..."; (iii) the high earning career had been practised "...over an appreciable period during the marriage [or civil partnership]..." (and this would need to be evidenced); (iv) a periodical payments award would be made "...towards the top end of the discretionary bracket applicable for a needs assessment... Compensation ought not to be reflected by a premium or additional element on top of the needs-based award..."[52]

Mostyn J has attempted to place substantial limitations on the compensation principle, by drawing on post-*Miller* authorities, but does acknowledge that he is bound by the House of Lords decision. The fourth strand of the test, in particular, would appear to be at odds with the judgment of Lady Hale, in *Miller*.[53]

In *RC v JC* [2020] **EWHC 466**, Moor J made a capital compensation award to a wife, where her application was supported by strong evidence and there was capital sufficient enough to exceed the parties' needs. The wife received £400,000 for sacrificing her legal career for the benefit of the family, in circumstances where it was clear that she had given up a

---

[51] *VB v JP* [2008] EWHC 112 (Fam); note that the Court of Appeal, in *H v H* [2014] EWCA Civ 1523, considered the judgment of Sir Mark Potter P to be key: *"...the full text of the judgment deserves careful consideration if and when the issue of compensation comes to be considered by this court." per* Ryder LJ at [40]

[52] *SA v PA (Pre-Marital Agreement: Compensation)* [2014] EWHC 392 at [36]

[53] *Miller; McFarlane, supra,* at [140]

"very good chance"[54] of being a partner. However, the judge cautioned that compensation claims would be made out only in the most exceptional of cases:

> "…litigants should think long and hard before launching a claim for relationship generated disadvantage and they should not take this judgment as any sort of "green light" to do so unless the circumstances are truly exceptional."[55]

It would appear that to succeed in being awarded a compensation element it is essential for there to have been some disadvantage suffered by the party claiming it, such that their career would have produced for them resources more substantial than the award that would be made. It is for the court to determine, separately, whether compensation should form part of an award so as to ensure that the outcome is fair to both parties, and if so, how. Notwithstanding the decision in *RC v JC*, it is extremely rare to succeed on a compensation claim.

Ringfencing Assets and the 'White Leopard'

In some cases, a party may seek to ringfence non-matrimonial, or 'separate', property. The Court of Appeal has confirmed that, "…the sharing principle applies with force to matrimonial property but does not apply, or applies with significantly less force, to non-matrimonial property…"[56] ; however, whilst sharing non-matrimonial property is said to be "…as rare as a white leopard…"[57], it is unlikely to be ringfenced where the assets remaining in the pot are insufficient to meet the parties' needs. It is therefore necessary to identify the matrimonial and non-matrimonial assets. Sometimes it is obvious which type of asset falls into either category, but other times it is not.

---

[54] *RC v JC* [2020] EWHC 466 at [67]

[55] *RC v JC, supra,* at [72]

[56] *Hart v Hart*, supra, *per* Moylan LJ at [62]

[57] *JL v SL (No 2)* [2015] EWHC 360 (Fam), *per* Mostyn J at [22]

As confirmed by Moylan LJ in ***Hart v* Hart [2017] EWCA Civ 1306**[58], there is no single route to determining what assets are marital. Two 'approaches' have been said to exist: the 'arithmetical approach' and the 'impressionistic approach'.[59] The former, applied by the Court of Appeal in *Jones*[60], requires the assets to be first divided into matrimonial and non-matrimonial assets. Those that are non-matrimonial are simply removed from the matrimonial pot, and the remaining assets are divided equally between the parties. When applying the latter approach, the nature and quality of the non-matrimonial assets will be factored into the court's discretionary exercise and a fair division of assets will be made. However, following the Court of Appeal's judgment in *Versteegh*,[61] quoting *Hart*[62] with approval, in fact it has been decided that the 'two principles' are "...examples of the same principle being applied, but applied in a different manner depending on the circumstances of the case..."[63]

In *Hart*, Moylan LJ further stated, "...the court does not have to apply any particular mathematical or other specific methodology. The court has a discretion as to how to arrive at a fair division and can simply apply a broad assessment of the division which would affect "overall fairness"..."[64] It is clear that each case will turn on its own facts, and the extent to which the relevant section 25 factors impact on the court's discretionary exercise will vary from case to case.

---

58 Referenced by Moylan LJ in *Martin v Martin* [2018] EWCA Civ 2866

59 *Versteegh v Versteegh* [2018] EWCA Civ 1050

60 *Jones v Jones* [2011] EWCA Civ 41

61 *Versteegh v Versteegh, supra*

62 *Versteegh v Versteegh, supra, per* Lady Justice King at [95]

63 *Hart v Hart, per* Moylan LJ at [87]

64 *Hart v Hart, supra, per* Moylan LJ at [96]

Defining matrimonial assets

When looking to categorise an asset, the source of it and the extent to which it has been 'mingled'[65] with family finances is highly relevant, as is the degree to which the family has become accustomed to it. Parties' perceptions often differ as to the extent of 'mingling' of an asset with a non-matrimonial source and there are often competing arguments as to whether all – or some – of it should continue to be viewed as non-matrimonial property. Such arguments undoubtedly often result in protracted litigation; one party asserts a sharing claim whilst the other is seeking for particular assets to be excluded from division. It may well be a costly (and risky) argument for parties to have, albeit often litigated upon in light of the court's overarching discretionary approach.

The longer the marriage and, often, the greater the length of time since the asset was received, the more likely it is to be considered to have become matrimonial. Sometimes, assets are considered to have both a matrimonial and a non-matrimonial element. Once an asset is viewed as being matrimonial, it is far less likely it is that it will be ringfenced. In any event, even if an asset retains its non-matrimonial character the asset will invariably have to be invaded so as to meet needs, if the parties' needs cannot be met without recourse to it.

A key area of dispute in many cases is the extent of the housing needs of each party. This is particularly relevant in cases where a non-matrimonial asset exists, which ought only to be invaded so as to meet needs. Often the parties will seek to convince the court that their own housing needs are higher than the other party deems them to be. The court will therefore be tasked with assessing property particulars, whilst having regard to (but not necessarily replicating) the standard of living during the marriage.

It is important to note that *all* property, whether matrimonial or non-matrimonial will be taken into account by the court as part of the court's

---

[65] *Charman v Charman (No 4)* [2007] EWCA Civ 503 at [46]

discretionary exercise.[66] Although any non-matrimonial property would not generally be subject to the sharing principle, it will be viewed as a financial resource[67] available to the party who owns it.

The family home is generally regarded as a matrimonial asset (whether or not the property is in joint names) and inherited assets or gifts are, usually, non-matrimonial. However, non-matrimonial assets can often lose their 'non-matrimonial' status as a result of the way in which they are treated within the marriage. Business assets, which have been brought to the marriage by one party, may bring another level of complexity to the concept of defining the nature of property, given that often a business value increases during the course of a marriage. The extent to which the marriage (the passage of time during the marriage, alongside the support or efforts of the other spouse) has contributed to that growth may be a relevant consideration.

Property brought into the marriage by one spouse and inherited property, whenever acquired[68], will generally be viewed as non-matrimonial property, albeit the significance of its non-matrimonial character diminishes over time.[69] A short marriage is unlikely to generate sharing in respect of non-matrimonial assets (unless the parties' needs require it) as this may well be unfair.[70]

The source of an inherited or gifted asset, for example, naturally leads it to be *prima facie* viewed as non-matrimonial in nature. However, this is not always clear cut. This is particularly so where the person who received the inheritance has (for example) used the money to reduce or redeem the mortgage on the family home, support the family generally, or has kept the inherited funds in a joint account. The waters can become muddied as to the extent to which the inherited assets should be regarded

---

66 *Norris v Norris* [2002] EWHC 2996 *per* Bennett J

67 Section 25(2)(a), MCA 1973

68 *White v White, supra*

69 *Miller/McFarlane, per* Lady Hale at [123]

70 *Miller, supra, per* Lord Nicholls at [24]

as matrimonial property and it could be implied that the receiving party intended for an inheritance to become matrimonial[71]. Such circumstances may result in a dispute between parties as to whether the asset should be up for division between the parties upon their separation.

In a slightly different category, business assets (initially brought into the marriage by one party) can be seen by the business owner as being exclusively theirs; however, if the business has been built up by one party whilst the other supports the party in achieving that business growth, perhaps by being responsible for the practical care of the children and the home, it would not be uncommon for the court to view the business (and its value) as a joint venture. It may also be the case that the non-business owner spouse or civil partner has carried out work in the business (and/or they are shareholders) and they may well regard the business as being matrimonial in nature in light of this.

As previously observed, pensions are a different class of asset to other capital assets. It is often argued that pre-marital (and sometimes post-separation) accruals should be ringfenced. The case of *W v H*[72] criticised an established practice that existed in some courts to simply make a straight-line deduction from the CE (cash equivalent value) of a relevant pension to reflect the fact that some of the pension was said to have been accrued outside of the marriage. The judge pointed out that, as with other classes of assets, the parties' needs must be taken into consideration and to ignore retirement income needs would be contrary to established authorities in respect of other assets. The PAG Report was quoted with approval:

> "…it is important to appreciate in needs-based cases, just as is the case with non-pension assets, the timing and the source of the pension saving is not necessarily relevant… It is clear from authority that in a needs case, the court can have resort to any

[71] *N v F* [2011] 2 FLR 533 at para 44

[72] *W v H, supra*

> assets, whenever required, in order to ensure the parties needs are appropriately met."[73]

It is of note that *W v H* was deemed to be a 'needs' case and the pensions up for division in that case amounted to just over £2 million.

The role of a nuptial agreement

As can be seen, whilst the authorities suggest that the sharing of non-matrimonial property is "…as rare as a white leopard…"[74] there may be inherent difficulties in identifying what constitutes the matrimonial 'pot', up for division, where there is a dispute about the assets that might fall to be considered to be non-matrimonial in nature. The level of discord between the parties, created by ongoing arguments about the extent of the matrimonial assets, may be increased and the parties prevented from achieving a final conclusion to their divorce, sometimes, for many years which is unlikely to be in the interests of the parties (or their children).

A financial settlement can, of course, be agreed between the parties post-separation and the terms can be entered into a consent order and submitted to a court for approval; however, there may often be a significant degree of acrimony which will make reaching an agreement inherently difficult. Even if a separation is generally amicable, it is likely the parties will have had to engage in some form of post-separation litigation (or at the very least negotiations) during an emotionally challenging time. The financial cost of resolving the financial provision on divorce or dissolution could be significant, and the emotional cost is often far greater.

Many people enter into pre-nuptial (or post-nuptial) agreements so as to attempt to retain a degree of control over the way in which their finances will be treated in the event of a divorce or dissolution (naturally subject to the court's endorsement). Parties are able to set out their intentions

---

73 *W v H* at [61], quoting p 22 of the PAG Report

74 *JL v SL (No 2)* [2015] EWHC 360, *per* Mostyn J at [22]

and record their mutual understanding as to how their finances will be treated, both within and outside of their marriage or civil partnership.

As nuptial agreements are not contractually binding in England and Wales, being a discretionary jurisdiction, some parties may be cautious about forming one. However, there is potentially a far greater scope for uncertainty and discord where no pre-nuptial or post-nuptial agreement exists. A nuptial agreement that is well-considered and carefully drafted should serve to limit post-separation litigation and reduce the financial and emotional burden.

CHAPTER THREE

BEFORE RADMACHER

This chapter provides an overview of the court's approach to nuptial agreements before the Supreme Court's landmark decision.

***

In 2010, the landscape on pre-nuptial and post-nuptial agreements changed in the jurisdiction of England and Wales. In ***Radmacher v Granatino*** **[2010] UKSC 42**, the Supreme Court held that where a valid nuptial agreement exists, it will generally be inferred that the parties intended to be bound by the terms of the agreement. Prior to outlining the Supreme Court decision, it is useful to have an understanding of the law relating to nuptial agreements, and key developments, leading up to *Radmacher*.[1]

Public Policy

Prior to the *Radmacher* decision, parties may have been advised that their agreement would hold little weight in this jurisdiction as nuptial agreements were void for public policy reasons. It was long-established that an agreement that contemplated or provided for the separation of a husband and wife at a future time was unlawful,[2] contrary to public policy and therefore void. Nuptial agreements were seen to erode marriage values and threaten the sanctity of marriage and there was a concern that the existence of such an agreement could potentially encourage divorce. "Such encouragement was seen as inconsistent with

[1] *Radmacher (formerly Granatino) v Granatino* [2010] UKSC 42

[2] *N v N (Jurisdiction: Pre-Nuptial Agreement)* [1999] 2 FLR 745

the fundamental, life-long and enforceable obligation of husband and wife to live with one another." [3]

Shortly before the Supreme Court's decision in *Radmacher*, the Board of the Privy Council, in ***MacLeod v MacLeod***,[4] confirmed that such a rule was outdated, but only in respect of post-nuptial agreements. The Board sought to draw a distinction between ante-nuptial agreements (as then commonly referred) that were made prior to marriage, and post-nuptial agreements.

Shortly after the decision in *MacLeod*, the 'public policy' rule was eliminated by the Supreme Court in respect of both pre-nuptial and post-nuptial agreements. In *Radmacher*, it was said, at [52] (approving of the comments made in *MacLeod*)[5]:

> "We wholeheartedly endorse the conclusion of the Board… that the old rule that agreements providing for future separation are contrary to public policy is obsolete and should be swept away, for the reasons given by the Board. But for reasons that we shall explain, this should not be restricted to post-nuptial agreements. If parties who have made such an agreement, whether ante-nuptial or post-nuptial, then decide to live apart, we can see no reason why they should not be entitled to enforce their agreement…"[6]

In the case of ***NA v MA* [2006] EWHC 2900**, Baron J (the same judge who heard *Radmacher v Granatino*[7] at first instance), sitting in the High Court, made the following comments:

---

[3] *Radmacher v Granatino, supra*, per Lady Hale at [143]

[4] *MacLeod v MacLeod* [2008] UKPC 64

[5] *MacLeaod v MacLeod, supra*, at [38-39]

[6] *Radmacher v Granatino, supra*, at [52]

[7] *Radmacher v Granatino, supra*

> "... for many years, agreements between spouses were considered void for public policy reasons but this is no longer the case. In fact, over the years, pre-nuptial 'contracts' have become increasingly common place and are, I accept, much more likely to be accepted by these courts as governing what should occur between the parties when the prospective marriage comes to an end. That is, of course, subject to the discretion of the court and the application of a test of fairness/manifest unfairness. It may well be that Parliament will provide legislation but, until that occurs, current authority makes it clear that the agreements are not enforceable per se, although they can be persuasive (or definitive) depending upon the precise circumstances that lead to their completion."[8]

The decision in *NA v MA* provides a useful indicator that there had already been a shift in the way the court was viewing the 'public policy' rule against nuptial agreements.

Developing Case Law

A shift in perspective was emerging. Here follows a chronological summary of the key cases. Given the old public policy rule that nuptial agreements were unlawful, the principles in the older cases were established in relation to separation agreements, but the same principles have evolved to now apply to nuptial agreements.

The House of Lords established, almost a century ago, in the case of ***Hyman v Hyman* [1929] AC 601**, which concerned a separation agreement, that spousal maintenance cannot be precluded from an agreement and that an agreement cannot purport to oust the jurisdiction of the court.[9] The court held that the existence of an agreement would constitute 'conduct that would be inequitable to disregard', under the applicable statutory provision that was equivalent to section 25 of the Matrimonial Causes Act 1973.

---

[8] NA v MA, *supra, per* Baron J, para 12; quoted in *Radmacher v Granatino* at [47]

[9] Confirmed in *Wright v Wright* [1970] 1 WLR 1219

In 1975, in a case involving a deed of separation, the Court of Appeal emphasised the importance of respect for adult autonomy, although it was said to be a "wholly exceptional case on the facts..."[10]

The Court of Appeal case of ***Edgar v Edgar* [1980] EWCA Civ 2** followed. This was a seminal case, as it upheld the terms of a separation agreement and provided clarity that adults' autonomous choice to enter into an agreement would be respected and accorded weight by the court, provided that certain safeguards are present and there are no vitiating factors.

The court gave guidance as to the requirements of an enforceable separation agreement, albeit in the years that have followed it has not been uncommon for judges to cite its terms as relevant to nuptial agreements. The following passage has a degree of familiarity, as against the principles ultimately established by *Radmacher*:

> "...To decide what weight should be given, in order to reach a just result, to a prior agreement not to claim a lump sum, regard must be had to the conduct of both parties leading up to the prior agreement, and to their subsequent conduct in consequence of it. It is not necessary in this connection to think in formal legal terms, search as misrepresentation or estoppel; all the circumstances as they affect each of two human beings must be considered in the complex relationship of marriage. So the circumstances surrounding the making of the agreement are relevant. Undue pressure by one side, exploitation of a dominant position to secure an unreasonable advantage, inadequate knowledge, possibly bad legal advice, an important change of circumstances, unforeseen or overlooked at the time of making the agreements, are all relevant to the question of justice between the parties. Important, too, is the general proposition that, formal agreements, properly and fairly arrived at with competent legal advice, should not be displaced unless there are good and substantial grounds for concluding that's an injustice will be done by holding the parties to the terms of their agreement..."[11]

---

[10] *Brockwell v Brockwell* [1975] CAT 75/468, Unreported, 5 November 1975

[11] *Edgar v Edgar* [1980] EWCA Civ 2, *per* Ormrod LJ at [893]

Fifteen years after *Edgar*, the case of ***F v F (Ancillary Relief: Substantial Assets)*** **[1995] 2 FLR 45** was decided. It concerned a husband seeking to enforce the terms of a pre-nuptial agreement, which (at that time) would have been contrary to public policy. The parties were German nationals. There were three children of the 11-year marriage. Two nuptial agreements had been created, but the one governed by German law was the one upon which the husband placed most reliance. The wife would have been held to the terms of the marital contract under German law, which sought to limit her claim to the equivalent of the pension of a German judge in a case with assets of around £150 million. The court held that the parties' contractual agreement could not oust the jurisdiction of the court, where statute prevails:

> "...the rights and responsibilities of those whose financial affairs are regulated by statute cannot be much influenced by contractual terms which were devised for the control and limitation of standards that are intended to be of universal application throughout our society.... I do not attach any significant weight to those contracts..."[12]

As a natural consequence of the rule that nuptial agreements were contrary to public policy, many of the cases involving pre-nuptial agreements involved foreign nationals. Several cases were simply remitted to the jurisdiction relevant to the facts of the case, with some remarks of the court suggesting there may be a degree of forum-shopping.

In ***N v N (Foreign Divorce: Financial Relief)*** **[1997] 1 FLR 900**, despite not making a final determination about the pre-nuptial agreement, the court took the opportunity to make an observation that a pre-nuptial agreement (which would have been binding in Sweden) would be "...no more than a material consideration in this court under section 25 of the Matrimonial Causes Act 1973..."[13]

---

[12] *F v F* per Thorpe LJ at p 66

[13] *N v N (Foreign Divorce: Financial Relief)* [1997] 1 FLR 900 *per* Cazalet J at pp912-913

The case of ***S v S (Matrimonial Proceedings: Appropriate Forum)*** **[1997] 1 WLR 1200**, involving a New York pre-nuptial agreement, was remitted to New York but the court expressed caution about the fact of attributing no significant weight to a pre-nuptial agreement, whatever the circumstances, particularly where the agreement was created in another jurisdiction where it would otherwise be binding. Wilson J predicted that a case would come, whereby the circumstances of the case would lead to a court finding a pre-nuptial agreement to be "...influential or even crucial..."[14] and highlighted that where other jurisdictions have been persuaded that justice demands parties should be held to the terms of their pre-nuptial agreements, the jurisdiction of England and Wales should be careful about too emphatically asserting the opposite, particularly in view of the fact that the judge "...could find nothing in section 25 to compel a conclusion so much at odds with [the] personal freedoms..." of autonomous, fully informed adults. The comments made by Wilson J, in *S v S*, were quite revolutionary in view of the old public policy rule and may have paved the way for a change in attitude towards nuptial agreements.

N v N (Jurisdiction: Pre-Nuptial Agreement) **[1999] 2 FLR 745** concerned a pre-nuptial agreement which was not enforced on public policy grounds. It was confirmed that there were no reported cases that enforced the terms of a pre-nuptial agreement. The court did, however, point out that the fact of nuptial agreements being unenforceable did not mean the parties would not be held to the terms of the agreement in appropriate circumstances, where justice demanded it.[15] The court cited *Edgar v Edgar*[16] in support of the proposition, even though *Edgar* related to a separation agreement.

The case of ***C v C (Divorce: Stay of English Proceedings)*** **[2001] 1 FLR 694** concerned a French couple who had entered into a pre-nuptial

[14] *S v S (Matrimonial Proceedings: Appropriate Forum)* [1997] 1 WLR 1200, *supra,* per Wilson J at pp 1203 – 1204

[15] *N v N (Jurisdiction: Pre-Nuptial Agreement)* [1999] 2 FLR 745 *per* Wall J at [42]

[16] *Edgar v Edgar, supra*

agreement. The wife had issued proceedings in England and there were concurrent proceedings, issued by the husband, in France. The court considered the case ought to be remitted to France, as the parties had made a positive and joint decision to enter an agreement in France, electing that the agreement should be determined according to French law.

M v M (Pre-Nuptial Agreement) [2002] 1 **FLR 654** was significant at the time because the pre-nuptial agreement was accorded weight. Both parties were Canadian nationals. The parties' circumstances were described as 'unusual'; there was an unplanned pregnancy, the husband did not want to marry (having had a previous acrimonious divorce) and the wife wanted to marry because of the unborn child (and contemplated abortion if there was no marriage). The husband insisted on a pre-nuptial agreement. Two lawyers refused to represent the wife due to a lack of financial disclosure and a third lawyer advised the wife not to sign the agreement, considering the agreement to be unfair. The wife insisted she wanted to enter the agreement, notwithstanding the advice, because she wanted to marry. The court held that the existence of a pre-nuptial agreement could be regarded as either 'one of the circumstances of the case' or 'conduct it would be inequitable to disregard'; either approach would accord weighing the very important factor of a pre-nuptial agreement into the statutory discretionary exercise.

Ultimately the court held that it would be unjust to the husband if the wife were not held to the terms of the agreement. An award was made to the wife in excess of that which the terms provided for, but only insofar as was necessary to meet her needs. The existence of the agreement made a difference to division that would otherwise have been made. This was an early indication that the court would be willing to accord weight to a nuptial agreement in the right circumstances, subject to 'needs'.

The case of *K v K (Ancillary Relief: Pre-Nuptial Agreement)* [2003] 1 **FLR 120** is a particularly useful reference for practitioners, as the judge helpfully produced a checklist of questions which he considered ought to be addressed when determining the fairness (or otherwise) of a pre-nuptial agreement. Although the decision pre-dates *Radmacher*, the checklist may be found to be a beneficial aide memoire for those drafting an agreement.[17]

The parties in *K v K* had a pre-nuptial agreement. It was a short marriage of 14 months to the date of separation. The parties were surprised by an unplanned pregnancy. In the circumstances, the wife wanted to marry and informed the husband that she would have an abortion if they did not. The husband was vehemently opposed to abortion and agreed they should get married.

After initially agreeing to marry, the husband called the engagement off saying he did not think the parties were ready. This prompted the wife's family to threaten to take the wife for a termination of the pregnancy but eventually the wife's father arranged for a pre-nuptial agreement to be drafted, which the parties signed. The husband was the wealthier party, although the wife was unaware of the true extent of his wealth. It transpired that the husband's asset base was somewhere in the region of £25 million. The wife also benefitted from family wealth and was purported to have assets equivalent to around £1 million. During divorce proceedings, the husband sought to rely upon the agreement and the wife sought to depart from it.

The parties had each received independent legal advice and the agreement provided that the wife would receive £100,000 if the marriage ended within five years. The husband would also make reasonable provision for any children. The marriage ended shortly after one year.

Rodger Hayward-Smith QC, sitting as a High Court Judge, found the pre-nuptial agreement to be fair, but increased the lump sum payable to the wife to £120,000 (which was in accordance with the husband's open offer). It was held that it would be unfair to the husband if the parties were not held to the agreement, given the circumstances leading up to their entering it.

---

[17] *K v K (Ancillary Relief: Pre-nuptial Agreement)* [2003] 1 FLR 120, pp 131 – 132

The case of *K v K* was decided around eight years before the Supreme Court handed down its *Radmacher* judgment and is a good illustration of the changing stance in respect of the public policy view of pre-nuptial agreements. However, the questionable background circumstances, including pressure upon the husband to marry prior to the agreement being put in place, may have considerably influenced the court's decision. Undoubtedly a major consideration for the court would have been the short duration of marriage, but, nonetheless, the background circumstances pertaining to the signing of the agreement were highly relevant and it would have been manifestly unfair on the husband to not hold the wife to the agreement. It is clear that this was an 'unusual'[18] set of circumstances.

When determining the issue of fairness, as against the checklist of factors, questions were posed by the judge in the following terms:

- Did the wife understand the agreement?
- Was she properly advised as to its terms?
- Did the husband put her under any pressure to sign the agreement?
- Was there full disclosure?
- Was the wife under any other pressure?
- Did she willingly sign the agreement?
- Did the husband exploit a dominant position, either financially or otherwise?
- Was the agreement entered into in the knowledge that there would be a child?
- Have any unforeseen circumstance arisen since the agreement was made that would make it just to hold the parties to it?
- What does the agreement mean? Is it clear?

[18] *M v M (Pre-nuptial Agreement)* [2002] 1 FLR 654, *per* Connell J

- Does the agreement preclude an order for periodical payments for the wife?
- Are there any grounds for concluding that an injustice would be done by holding the parties to the terms of the agreement?
- Is the agreement one of the circumstances of the case to be considered under section 25 of the Matrimonial Causes Act 1973?
- Does the entry into this agreement constitute conduct which it would be inequitable to disregard under section 25(2)(g) of the Matrimonial Causes Act 1973?
- Am I breaking new ground by holding the wife to the capital terms of the agreement?
- Would it be unjust to hold the parties to the agreement if it precludes a claim for periodical payments?

The answers the judge provided to the questions are not set out in full here, however, the following key findings of the court are worthy of note:

- There was disclosure, albeit not full disclosure. However, the decision not to press for asset values came from the wife's side and it was known the husband was very wealthy (the judge stated that figures in excess of his actual wealth were mentioned by the wife's father).
- Both parties were found to be under pressure. Although the agreement was signed the day before the wedding, the terms of the agreement had been discussed and agreed before then and the wife had had plenty of time to consider the terms.
- The court held that an injustice would be done to the husband if the agreement were to be ignored.
- The very fact of the parties entering the agreement amounted to conduct which it would be inequitable to disregard.

It is of note that the court's treatment of the nuptial agreement in *K v K* is not dissimilar to the Court of Appeal's approach in the post-*Radmacher* case of *Versteegh v Versteegh*[19]. In *Versteegh*, the court found there to be a valid agreement and did not consider that the husband's departure from the terms of the agreement (by making a more generous offer than the agreement would have otherwise provided for the wife) negated the whole agreement.

In ***J v V (Disclosure: Offshore Corporations)*** **[2004] 1 FLR 1042**, the pre-nuptial agreement was regarded, by Coleridge J, as being of no significance. The contract was "… signed on the very eve of the marriage, without full legal advice, without proper disclosure and it made no allowance for the arrival of children."[20] The circumstances surrounding the making of the agreement were such that the court went on to further state that the terms of the agreement were "…obviously unfair…"[21] and thus the nuptial agreement was not accorded any weight.

In ***G v G (Financial Provision: Separation Agreement)*** **[2004] 1 FLR 1011**, the Court of Appeal, upheld the decision of the court of first instance to accord weight to the parties' pre-nuptial and separation agreements. The case involved parties who had experienced previous divorces and the court gave due regard to their autonomous choice to enter into such agreements. Although a pre-nuptial agreement was considered, the parties had subsequently chosen to enter a separation agreement, which the Court of Appeal had stated would generally be upheld (absent any vitiating factors) since *Edgar*.[22]

The case of ***NA v MA*** **[2006] EWHC 2900**[23] is an important case. It was quoted with approval in *Radmacher* and was also considered by the Law Commission in its 2014 recommendations. It demonstrates, factually, how undue pressure and exploitation of a dominant position might appear. The case involved a post-nuptial agreement, entered into after

---

19 *Versteegh v Versteegh* [2018] EWCA Civ 1050

20 *J v V (Disclosure: Offshore Corporations)* [2004] 1 FLR 1042, at [41]

21 *J v V, supra,* at [41]

22 *Edgar v Edgar, supra*

23 Also known as *A v A*

the husband had discovered the wife's adultery. The wife was coerced into signing the nuptial agreement, by the husband, because he said that if she did not enter into such an agreement he would divorce her. Ultimately the parties did separate and divorce; however, in the circumstances surrounding the execution of it, the court held it would not be fair for the court to attribute any weight to the agreement whatsoever. Baron J, the judge in *Radmacher* at first instance, set out the (then present) law on pre-nuptial agreements.[24]

Ella v Ella **[2007] EWCA Civ 99** attracted jurisdictional consideration. It involved an Israeli pre-nuptial agreement and there were concurrent proceedings in Israel. The court at first instance granted a stay of the proceedings, given that the pre-nuptial agreement clearly stated the law of Israel should apply to any financial proceedings. The Court of Appeal stated the court of first instance was correct to remit the case to Israel, notwithstanding the wife's contention that there were vitiating factors attending to the making of the agreement.

The Court of Appeal considered an application for permission to appeal, followed by the substantive appeal, in the case of ***Crossley v Crossley*** **[2007] EWCA Civ 1491**. There was a pre-nuptial agreement, which provided that the parties' pre-acquired, respective assets should be kept separate. Notably, this was a short marriage of only 14 months and the parties each brought significant wealth to the marriage: the husband £45 million and the wife a not insignificant sum of £18 million. The Court of Appeal gave permission to appeal but the wife's appeal, based on the premise that the husband had not provided full disclosure, was ultimately not successful.

The Court of Appeal in *Crossley* held that, where the right circumstances exist, the existence of a pre-nuptial agreement could be a 'factor of magnetic importance':

[24] Full text produced earlier in this Chapter

> "...All these cases are fact dependent and this is a quite exceptional case on its facts, but if ever there is to be a paradigm case in which the court will look to the prenuptial agreement as not simply one of the peripheral factors in the case but as a factor of magnetic importance, it seems to me that this is just such a case."[25]

For the first time, the Court of Appeal had confirmed that a pre-nuptial agreement could well be determinative. It will be noted that this was a very short marriage and one where the court did not have to assess 'needs', given the significant resources involved.

As dealt with at the beginning of this Chapter, the Privy Council case of ***MacLeod v MacLeod*** **[2010] UKPC 64** was a key stepping-stone towards the Supreme Court's decision in *Radmacher*. The case concerned a post-nuptial agreement, which, incidentally, contained some terms from a pre-nuptial agreement. The agreement failed to provide for the needs of the parties' five children and it was held the agreement should have done, so the case was remitted to the High Court for an assessment of quantum in this regard. Otherwise, the post-nuptial agreement was valid and the parties were held to the remainder of its terms.

The Privy Council sought to draw a distinction between pre-nuptial and post-nuptial agreements, stating that the latter would be enforceable, whereas the former would not. It was suggested that the public policy rule was outdated and should not apply to post-nuptial agreements. Of course, shortly afterwards, *Radmacher* approved of sweeping away the old public policy rule but confirmed a solid belief that the rule should be eradicated in respect of all nuptial agreements, whether pre or post marriage.

At the time the High Court heard the appeal in ***F v S (Pre-nuptial Agreement)*** **[2009] EWHC 2485 (Fam)**[26], *Radmacher* had already been heard in the Court of Appeal. The parties in *F v S* had a pre-nuptial

[25] *Crossley v Crossley per* Thorpe LJ at [15]

[26] Also known as *F v F*

agreement, which was signed in France. It was a standard 'separation of property' agreement, drafted in French by a French lawyer, although the parties were married in Switzerland. The court held that the parties had travelled to France to sign the agreement prior to their wedding on the understanding that it was a document that was required under French law and therefore no more than an administrative requirement. The court held that the parties could not be said to have a full appreciation of the terms and implications, due to the fact that neither party knew the notary or had any understanding of the legal principles upon which the agreement was based. The court accordingly attributed no weight to the agreement when carrying out its section 25 exercise.

***

As can be seen, gradually the courts were acceding to a position whereby pre-nuptial agreements were no longer viewed as contrary to public policy and they were being regarded as relevant (and sometimes determinative) factors within the court's discretionary exercise. This contributed to the supposedly seismic revolution in the Supreme Court. Perhaps it should not have been such a surprise in light of the history of the case law, but that is easy to infer with the benefit of hindsight.

CHAPTER FOUR

RADMACHER V GRANATINO

This chapter provides a summary of the development of the case of *Radmacher v Granatino*, from first instance to the Supreme Court: the key facts, decisions, appeals and the ultimate judgment.

> **"The court should give effect to a nuptial agreement that is freely entered into by each party with a full appreciation of its implications unless in the circumstances prevailing it would not be fair to hold the parties to their agreement."**
>
> *Radmacher v Granatino* [2010] UKSC 42 at [75]

Facts[1]

The parties were Katrin Radmacher (formerly Granatino) and Nicolas Granatino. Ms Radmacher (the wife) is a German national and Mr Granatino (the husband) is a French national. The parties met in 1997, when the husband was aged 26 and the wife was aged 28. They married on 28 November 1998, after becoming engaged and commencing cohabitation in June 1998.

The parties lived as husband and wife in England, having married in London in 1998 and (save for a short period of living in New York) remained living there until separation in 2006. There were two children of the family, aged nine and six, at the date the judgment of first instance

[1] Facts taken from the three reported judgments of *Radmacher (formerly Granatino) v Granatino*: [2008] EWCA Civ 1304 (permission to appeal hearing); [2009] EWCA Civ 649 (Court of Appeal); [2010] UKSC 42 (Supreme Court)

was given, on 28 July 2008. It was a marriage of approximately 8.5 years, from seamless cohabitation.

The wife was very wealthy, with liquid assets equivalent to £54 million, purportedly comprised of £33 million in Credit Suisse, £19 million in UBS and £2 million with the Fortis Bank in Dublin. She also had significant minority interests in two valuable family companies, which the court found to be so substantial that her interests generated an annual income of some circa £2 million net. Her wealth was entirely inherited.

The husband had virtually no assets. Although he had started the marriage with a career as an investment banker, earning circa £50,000 initially and increasing to circa £120,000 by the date of marriage. In 2003 the husband quit his job in the City and began conducting research in biotechnology at Oxford University. The savings the husband had generated through his investment banking career were spent on the family over the two years following his departure from his job and, by the time of the permission to appeal hearing (3 October 2008), he had amassed significant debt, partly as a result of the litigation surrounding the breakdown of the parties' relationship.

Pre-Nuptial Agreement

The key factor for consideration was the pre-nuptial agreement, which was signed on 1 August 1998 (almost four months prior to the marriage). The wife's father insisted the parties enter a pre-marital contract. The wife reported that she would be disinherited if the parties did not enter into such an agreement.

Shortly after their engagement, on 6 July 1998, the wife's mother instructed a notary in Germany, to draft a pre-marital agreement which provided for a separation of property: that neither party would make a claim on the other in the event of a divorce. The notary was concerned that this could leave the wife in difficulty, particularly given the husband's 'excellent' income at the time. The wife's mother informed the notary that there would be no risk to her daughter in any event because she had a significant annual income, plus the benefit of other monies.

The notary followed up the discussion with the wife, on the same day, and she confirmed the instructions. At the insistence of the notary, it was agreed the pre-nuptial agreement would be drafted as soon as possible, so as to give the husband an opportunity to understand it (including obtaining a translation) and to seek legal advice upon it.

A first draft of the pre-nuptial agreement, in German, was sent to the wife for her consideration on 17 July 1998. It contained a clause for the parties to detail the approximate values of their assets. The wife contacted the notary, by telephone, and asked for this to be removed, as the parties would provide that information to each other separately, outside of the agreement.

A second draft was produced and, upon the wife's instructions, sent to the wife's father. On 23 July 1998, the wife advised that her father sought additional clauses preventing the husband from inheriting company shares, directly or indirectly (i.e. through any children of the marriage). Following advice, it was agreed this was to be dealt with in the wife's will.

The final draft was sent to the wife on 24 July 1998; it was still in German and no translation had been provided to the husband. Whilst the basic terms of the agreement were made clear to him, the husband was not informed that the notary wanted the agreement to be translated into a language convenient for him in order that he could have an opportunity to properly consider the agreement and obtain independent legal advice.

The parties attended the notary's office in order to execute the agreement on 1 August 1998. The notary was angry at the lack of translation. When, as found by the court, the husband informed the notary that he had seen the draft agreement but had not been provided with a translation of it, the notary considered the deficiency to be of such importance that he suggested the parties should delay signing the agreement until such time as the husband could have a proper opportunity to consider the terms in a language he could understand. The notary was, however, persuaded to continue when the parties informed him that they were unlikely to be in Germany again before the marriage ceremony.

The parties were taken through the agreement, by the notary, who spoke in English. Although he did not provide a verbatim translation, he described the terms clearly and in detail. The agreement was executed by the parties that day. Two days later, the notary wrote to the parties stressing the importance of taking the advice of a local lawyer before taking up permanent residence in another jurisdiction (i.e. the UK, as planned).

Pre-marital contracts are contractually binding in both Germany and France. Despite the reservations of the notary, the husband did not take advantage of the postponement suggested. He also did not seek independent legal advice in the intervening months, between the execution of the pre-marital contract and the marriage ceremony.

The court at first instance found that the wife did not make it obvious that it was her that was demanding the agreement be signed as a pre-condition of marriage. Baron J also found that the husband was eager to sign the agreement because he wanted to marry and wanted to ensure the wife was not disinherited; he was unable to perceive any circumstances where he would want to make a claim.

The court found it was "highly unlikely"[2] that the wife had shown the first draft of the agreement to the husband, but it was not accepted that the husband had not seen a draft at all, finding that the husband had seen the final draft, which was available from 24 July 1998.

Proceedings

First Instance Decision

The High Court judgment was handed down on 28 July 2008. Baron J did accept the unchallenged expert evidence that the pre-nuptial agreement would be fully enforced against the husband in both Germany

[2] *Radmacher (formerly Granatino) v Granatino* [2010] UKSC 42 at [90] (hereafter, within this Chapter, "*Radmacher* SC")

and France but the learned judge attributed very little weight to the pre-nuptial agreement, citing the following reasons:[3]

(i) the husband had no independent legal advice;

(ii) it deprives the husband of all claims 'to the furthest permissible legal extent' and, given the events that had occurred, it would be manifestly unfair to hold the husband to the terms of the agreement;

(iii) the wife had given no disclosure of the extent of her resources;

(iv) there had been no negotiations between the parties or their representatives;

(v) the arrival of children had changed the landscape so much that the agreement ought to be disregarded.

A final order was made in the following terms:

- The wife to pay to the husband a lump sum of £5,560,000[4] within 3 days, by 31 July 2008.
- The lump sum to be paid from the wife's accounts with UBS.
- The lump sum to carry interest at the judgment debt rate.
- The wife would be required to continue to comply with the order for interim maintenance (dated 15.07.2007) until payment of the lump sum; any payments made after 31.07.2008 should be credited against interest due in respect of the lump sum.

[3] *Radmacher* SC at [110]

[4] Comprised of £2.5 m for a home in London; £25,000 to buy a car; £2.335 m as a capitalised Duxbury fund; £700,000 towards the husband's debts, which were then £800,000 (the £100,000 difference said to be the *"best estimate of the costs of the husband's fruitless application to challenge the order permitting the relocation of the children to Germany"* – Court of Appeal judgment: [2009] EWCA Civ 649 at [39])

- Child maintenance to be paid by the wife to the husband (for substantial periods when the children are staying with the husband) at the rate of £35,000 per annum, for each child.
- The wife to fund the purchase of a property in Germany for the children and the husband, as their carer, (plus a small sum to furnish it), to remain available for their use until the children complete further education (a sum of 630,000) by 1 December 1998.

The judge made the award following an assessment of the husband's needs and having given some "reducing effect"[5] to the pre-nuptial contract (albeit both appellate courts later considered it was not apparent that any significant reduction in the award had been made). It was understood that £19 m of the wife's £54 m liquid capital lay in UBS accounts. It was affirmed that the wife had not made interim periodical payments to the husband, which had been ordered in July 2017.

The wife immediately requested permission to appeal, which was refused. She then requested a stay of execution pending the outcome of her request for permission to appeal; Baron J informed the wife that she could have a stay only if she made a payment for security[6], at which point the wife withdrew her application for a stay.

Intervening: Freezing Injunctions

The date for payment of the lump sum of £5.560 m came and passed and, at the permission to appeal hearing, the wife was said to have been in contempt of court. In August 2008, the husband obtained a freezing injunction (without notice) against the wife's UK assets and obtained mirror orders in Ireland and Switzerland, against assets held in those jurisdictions.

[5] *Radmacher (formerly Granatino) v Granatino* [2008] EWCA Civ 1304 at [5] (Permission to Appeal judgment)

[6] Permission to Appeal judgment: [2008] EWCA Civ 1304 at [5]

Unbeknown to the husband or the court (later discovered by the husband), the wife had written to Fortis Bank in Dublin on 23 July 2008 (five days before the first instance judgment was handed down) seeking to transfer all of her funds held with them. The transfer did not take place, due to a lack of a stock transfer form. On 29 August 2008, the Fortis Bank in Dublin wrote to the wife to explain that her request could not be completed as the freezing injunction had been received.

On or around 4 September 2008, the Swiss mirror order was served upon Credit Suisse and UBS. Credit Suisse acknowledged receipt but stated that the wife had emptied her accounts 'long before'. UBS acknowledged receipt of the Swiss mirror order but did not say whether any monies had been successfully frozen (note that UBS is the account from which the judge ordered the lump sum to be paid).

On 23 September 2008, the wife wrote to the Court of Appeal, stating that she was unable to pay the outstanding instalments due under the order as a result of the freezing injunction the husband had obtained. On 2 October 2008, the day before the permission to appeal hearing, the wife's solicitors wrote to the husband's requesting consent to vary the freezing order so that she could make the instalment payments due; the Court of Appeal later found this to be 'window dressing' for the permission to appeal hearing.

Permission to Appeal

The wife sought permission to appeal on all grounds. The Court of Appeal gave judgment on the permission application on 3 October 2008. The wife's application for permission was successful but the Court of Appeal made an order for security, as a pre-condition for the wife being granted permission to appeal, and made it clear that the said security was in order to secure a level playing field for the parties:

> "...it is clear that the wife wants to put herself into a win-win situation and that she does not wish to participate fairly in the English forensic process. She would prefer to win by securing success in her appeal but, if she is not to win by that route, then

> she proposes to win by doing everything possible – with the massive resources at her command, quite unmatched by any resources at that of the husband – to put her assets beyond the reach of this court... The wife has an arguable case to put to this court and I hope that she does so; but the only playing field which we provide here for public use is a level one. Thus my view is that we should attach a condition to the grant of permission whereby a sum of money should, within a specified period of time, be brought by the wife into a secure environment to abide the determination of the appeal..."[7]

The security comprised the lump sum ordered to have been paid by 31.08.2008, the accrued interest, the outstanding interim periodical payments and security for costs incurred by the husband. It also included the lump sum for the German property purchase, although it was not due until December 2008, because the Court of Appeal's view was "...that the conduct of the wife [between the first instance decision and the application for permission to appeal] gives rise to an inevitable inference that she does not intend to make that payment on 1 December 2008..."[8] The husband's proposed inclusion of security for capitalised child maintenance payments was rejected.

The Court of Appeal considered Mr Granatino's application for security for costs under Rule 25 of the CPR and found that the wife had "...taken steps in relation to her assets that would make it difficult to enforce an order for costs against her..."[9] such that the Court was "...satisfied, having regard to all the circumstances of the case, that it [was] just to make such an order..."[10] for security of costs.

---

[7] *Radmacher v Granatino* [2008] EWCA Civ 1304 (Permission to Appeal Hearing), *per* Wilson J at [24]

[8] *Radmacher v Granatino* [2008] EWCA Civ 1304 (Permission to Appeal Hearing), *per* Wilson J at [28]

[9] Rule 25.13(2)(g), Civil Procedure Rules

[10] Rule 25.13(1)(a), Civil Procedure Rules

The Court of Appeal

The appeal hearing was heard by Thorpe, Rix and Wilson LJJ on 27 April 2009 and judgment was handed down on 2 July 2009. The Court of Appeal allowed the wife's appeal, having found the judge's discretionary exercise to have been erroneous, stating "...despite the appearance of the ante-nuptial agreement as a factor, the overall impression is of a negligible resulting discount."[11] The judge should have given "...decisive weight to the contract in the exercise which she conducted under s.25..."[12]

The Court of Appeal varied the award made, tempering it so as to accord due weight to the pre-nuptial agreement that was entered into by the parties. However, instead of adjusting the quantum of the award, the Court of Appeal limited the housing fund and the income fund to Mr Granatino's needs in his role as a father, rather than as a husband.

The unanimous decision of the Court of Appeal was that the housing fund of £2.5 m should not be the husband's absolutely but should be a reversionary interest, held on trust until the youngest child is aged 22. Similarly, the capitalised spousal maintenance figure should not be a life interest but end upon the youngest child's 22nd birthday.

The Court of Appeal did not interfere with the additional capital award (in respect of the husband's liabilities and the car fund), the husband's need for a home in the place of the children's habitual residence or the award in respect of child periodical payments.

Thorpe LJ stated:

> "Due respect for adult autonomy suggests that, subject of course to proper safeguards, a carefully fashioned contract should be

[11] *Radmacher,* Court of Appeal, per Thorpe LJ [43]

[12] *Radmacher,* Court of Appeal, per Wilson LJ at [149]

> available as an alternative to the stress, anxieties and expenses of a submission to the width of the judicial discretion..."[13]

The Court's opinion was held "...on the following foundations:

(i) Any provision that seeks to oust the jurisdiction of the court will always be void but severable.

(ii) Any contract will be voidable if breaching proper safeguards or vitiated under general principles of the law of contract.

(iii) Any contract would be subject to the review of a judge exercising his duty under section 25 if asserted to be manifestly unfair to one of the contracting parties..."[14]

Rix LJ summarised the court's reasons for its determination on the facts as follows:

> "... this is a case in which the prenuptial agreement made by the parties should be given decisive weight in the section 25 exercise. Their agreement was entered into willingly and knowingly by responsible adults. The husband had a proper understanding of the consequences of his agreement. It is to be inferred that without that agreement no marriage would have taken place, and that the wife's father would not have made over to her the additional resources which followed her marriage. The parties entered into their agreement with the help and advice of a German lawyer, under German law, making an agreement which was familiar to the civil law under which both parties and their families had grown up in Germany and France. The husband had thereafter chosen his own course in life, and, in giving up his earlier career as a banker and becoming a student, has acted in what he has considered to be in his own best interests. Fortunately and because of his own considerable abilities, he has succeeded in his new direction in life. What the future will bring to him as an able scientist, academic or researcher remains to be seen, but he is doing exactly what he wants to do. The marriage has been blessed with children, and there is shared residence between the parents,

[13] *Radmacher,* Court of Appeal [27] per Thorpe LJ

[14] *Radmacher,* Court of Appeal [28] per Thorpe LJ

> but the pre-nuptial agreement in any event recognised that the interests of the children should stand outside the parents' agreement. The provision of a home for the husband and for his needs as a father, carer and home-maker for the children will, in the circumstances, more than adequately provide him with the means to support his own needs. There is no case for making that home and financial support his to command for the whole of his life-time. By the time the younger daughter is out of education or has reached 22, he will have had every opportunity to make his own life and to earn such a living as will reflect his own aspirations."[15]

Cross-Appeal

The husband made a cross-appeal in respect of the second home for which he had been awarded 630,000. During the first instance proceedings it was a settled position that the wife and children would live in Düsseldorf, Germany. Baron J, at first instance, therefore made an assessment of the appropriate housing fund on the basis of that location.

On 25 November 2008, only four months after the first instance decision (and two months after the Court of Appeal granted the wife permission to appeal), the wife announced that she and the children would be moving to Monaco: she had made the decision 10 days previously and they would be moving within the following three weeks; it was presented as *a fait accompli*. The husband's objection prompted the wife to make an application for permission to relocate to the Family Court equivalent in Düsseldorf. The court granted the wife permission to relocate on 28 May 2009 and she and the children relocated on 4 June 2009, approximately one month before the Court of Appeal handed down its judgment.

Given the considerable disparity in property values in Monaco as against Düsseldorf, the housing fund of 630,000 was found to be insufficient to meet the housing needs of the husband and the children in Monaco and would frustrate the husband's care of the children. As such, the Court of

[15] *Radmacher* Court of Appeal [81] per Rix LJ

Appeal both granted permission and allowed the husband's cross-appeal, solely on the basis of fresh evidence, and it was remitted to Baron J for an appropriate assessment of the quantum of the fund for the Monaco home.

The Supreme Court

Mr Granatino appealed to the Supreme Court, where the decision of the Court of Appeal was upheld, by a majority of eight to one.[16] Lord Phillips gave the leading judgment[17] and Lady Hale gave a detailed dissenting judgment.[18]

> **"...in future it will be natural to infer that parties who enter into an ante-nuptial agreement to which English law is likely to be applied intend that effect should be given to it..."**
>
> *per* Lord Phillips at [70]

The Supreme Court held that nuptial agreements, whether pre-nuptial or post-nuptial, should no longer be regarded as contrary to public policy. The court would be required to examine the circumstances leading to the creation of the nuptial agreement and, providing there are no vitiating factors and appropriate safeguards are met, the court will generally hold the parties to their agreement, subject to it being fair to do so, which invariably means ensuring the needs of the parties are met.

The Supreme Court made some key preliminary observations, upon which the final determination was made:

- "...the old rule that agreements providing for future separation are contrary to public policy is obsolete and should be swept

---

[16] Lord Phillips, Lord Hope, Lord Rodger, Lord Walker, Lady Hale, Lord Brown, Lord Mance, Lord Collins, Lord Kerr

[17] *Radmacher* SC [1 – 123]

[18] *Radmacher* SC [131 – 195]

away…" in respect of all nuptial agreements, whether pre-nuptial or post-nuptial.[19]

- The court is bound to have regard to nuptial agreements, whether or not they have contractual status, as the court retains the overall statutory discretion.[20] In such circumstances, it is unnecessary for agreements to be binding.[21]

- The court should apply the same principles, whether considering a pre-nuptial agreement or a post-nuptial agreement.[22]

In reaching its decision, the Supreme Court placed great emphasis on respecting individual autonomy, where the parties had freely entered an agreement with a full appreciation of its implications.[23] The court highlighted the elements that would be necessary for a valid nuptial agreement to exist.[24] These can be summarised as follows:

- The parties must exercise their own free will in entering the agreement and they must be informed of and understand the implications of the agreement.

- Each party should have all the information that is relevant to their decision: there should be no 'material' lack of disclosure, information or advice.

- Legal advice is desirable, as it will show that the implications of the agreement are understood; however, if a party chooses not to obtain legal advice that will not negate the agreement.

---

[19] *Radmacher* SC at [52]

[20] *Radmacher* SC at [62] (however, note the Law Commission recommendations and evidence of an intention to be bound by the terms of an agreement will assist in evidencing the parties' state of mind and level of understanding)

[21] *Radmacher* SC [69]

[22] *Radmacher* SC at [63]

[23] *Radmacher* SC at [75]

[24] *Radmacher* SC at [67 – 83]

- Full disclosure of assets may be necessary to ensure the party fully understands the implications of an agreement; however, the onus is upon the other party to seek disclosure. A clear indifference to disclosure will not diminish the weight attributed to an agreement.

- Each party should intend that the agreement should govern their financial arrangements, in the event of divorce or dissolution.

- There must be no duress, fraud or misrepresentation (their existence would negate the agreement).

- Unconscionable conduct, such as undue pressure, is likely to eliminate the weight attributable to a nuptial agreement.

- Unworthy conduct, such as exploitation of a dominant position to secure an unfair advantage, would reduce or eliminate the weight accorded to a nuptial agreement.

Once a valid nuptial agreement has been found to exist parties' autonomy to enter such an agreement should generally be respected, providing it is 'fair' to do so. The Supreme Court set out some features, which a court will be mindful of when determining whether it is fair to hold the parties to their agreement:

- The circumstances of the parties existing at the time of entering the agreement will be relevant, including: the parties' emotional state and any pressures they were under to sign the agreement; the parties age and maturity; whether either or both had been married or in a long-term relationship before; whether the marriage would have gone ahead without a pre-nuptial agreement (this may go either way).

- Nuptial agreements created in other jurisdictions will not generally be given enhanced weight due to their status as enforceable contracts, but the foreign element may serve to demonstrate the parties' intentions to be bound by the agreement terms.

- It must be 'fair' to hold the parties to their agreement, in the circumstances existing at the time of reliance upon it; this will be fact-specific.
- A nuptial agreement cannot prejudice the reasonable requirements of any children of the family.
- An agreement that attempts to address all future contingencies is less likely to be upheld, as it would be unfair to hold the parties to an agreement that provided for uncertain future circumstances.
- If needs are not met by implementing the terms of the nuptial agreement, it would be unfair to hold the parties to their agreement.
- It is not likely to be fair to hold the parties to an agreement, where the terms have the effect of depriving one party of wealth that has been earned and accumulated during the marriage or civil partnership in a traditional breadwinner / homemaker relationship.
- If both parties are in a position to meet their own needs, it is likely to be fair to hold the parties to their agreement.
- Of the three tenets of fairness, the sharing principle is the one most likely to be affected by a nuptial agreement (i.e. the parties may opt out of it).
- A nuptial agreement is one factor for consideration in the court's discretionary exercise, to which the court will attribute appropriate weight when considering 'all the circumstances of the case'.
- The nuptial agreement may be the most 'compelling' factor in the circumstances of the case and therefore given decisive weight.

The Supreme Court held that there is nothing inherently unfair in agreeing to ringfence non-matrimonial property.[25] The court should respect individual autonomy by attributing weight to a nuptial agreement.[26] It was made clear that the weight attributed to an agreement will be reduced, if the circumstances pertaining to the making of the agreement or its terms make it unfair, but the crucial consideration for the court will be "…whether the agreement operates unfairly having regard to the circumstances prevailing at the time of the breakdown of the marriage [or civil partnership]."[27] A change in circumstances would likely warrant the creation of a fresh agreement.

Lady Hale, who had been a member of the Board in *MacLeod*, gave a separate and full dissenting judgment in *Radmacher* and confirmed her view that post-nuptial and pre-nuptial agreements should continue to be treated differently.[28] Lady Hale stated that the decision in *MacLeod* had done no more than endorse the wording of the Matrimonial Proceedings and Property Act 1970, "…which also swept away the basis of [the] public policy rule…"[29]

It is apparent that Lady Hale considered the endorsement of the principle that pre-nuptial agreements are viewed as being on a par with post-nuptial agreements to be a retrograde step, particularly given that the courts had "…arrived at a position where the differing roles which either may adopt within the relationship are entitled to equal esteem…"[30] She cautioned that the court should not lose sight of the fact that "…the object of an ante-nuptial agreement is to deny the economically weaker spouse the provision to which she – it is usually although by no means invariably she – would otherwise be entitled…"[31] and highlighted the

25 *Radmacher* SC at [79]

26 *Radmacher* SC at [78]

27 *Radmacher* SC at [73]

28 *Radmacher* SC at [138]

29 *Radmacher* SC at [157]

30 *Radmacher*, per Lady Hale at [132]

31 *Radmacher* SC at [137]

fact of a "gender dimension"[32] to the issue that would be likely to disproportionately affect women.

However, given the development of case law, set out in Chapter 3, it is perhaps not so surprising that the Supreme Court "swept away" the old rule. [33]

Ultimately the Supreme Court endorsed the position that "...the courts are now much more ready to attribute the appropriate (and in the right case, decisive) weight to an agreement as part of 'all the circumstances of the case' [within the meaning of section 25(1) of the Act of 1973]..." and it is the court that decides what the appropriate "...quantification of the claim for financial relief [should be]... with the parties' agreement being but one factor in the process and perhaps, in the right case, it being the most compelling factor..."[34]

The Supreme Court outlined a significant change in the world of pre-nuptial agreements, which had, in the recent past, been void and considered contrary to public policy. Post *Radmacher*, valid nuptial agreements made before or within marriage would ordinarily be upheld subject always to the parties' needs[35], which will be assessed at the time of the financial settlement.

---

[32] *Radmacher* SC at [137]

[33] *Radmacher* SC at [52]

[34] *Radmacher* SC at [83]

[35] Note the post *Radmacher* Court of Appeal judgment in *Brack v Brack* [2018] EWCA Civ 2862, which confirmed that an award in excess of needs would not, as a matter of law, be precluded and that a fair result may, albeit unusually, demand an award in excess of needs; see also *Currie v Monastyrski* [2017] EWCA Civ 1790, where the extent of mixing of assets during the marriage meant that it would have been unfair to hold the parties to their nuptial agreement.

CHAPTER FIVE

COURTS IN RECENT YEARS I: THE COURT OF APPEAL

This chapter considers the main developments in reported Court of Appeal decisions relating to nuptial agreements, since ***Radmacher v Granatino***[1], providing an overview of the cases and the decisions made.

Appeal Hearings

The Court of Appeal first gave substantive consideration to a pre-nuptial agreement almost eight years after the Supreme Court's decision in *Radmacher.*

***Versteegh v Versteegh* [2018] EWCA Civ 105** involved a pre-marital agreement that was signed on the day before the wedding. There were three non-minor children of the 21-year marriage. The husband was an affluent businessman, and the wife was a homemaker. The case involved assets worth £273 million. Both parties were Swedish nationals, who had married in Sweden. The pre-marital agreement was a contractual arrangement which stated the parties would each retain their own assets, both acquired before and during the marriage.

Pre-marital agreements are commonplace in Sweden, with parties generally electing for marital assets to be subject to a regime of either community or separation of property. The wife did not obtain legal advice before signing the agreement. The husband's evidence was that that the parties had discussed the binding agreement and its terms in detail several months beforehand, whereas the wife said she had only read

[1] *Radmacher (formerly Granatino) v Granatino* [2010] UKSC 42

the agreement upon separation (21 years later) and was shocked to note its terms. However, a mutual friend of the parties gave evidence that the wife was fully aware of its implications. Of note, the husband's open offer was more generous than would have been provided for had the terms of the pre-marital agreement been observed.

At first instance (Sir Peter Singer):

The court found the wife to have deliberately lied about her level of understanding. She was found to have been fully aware of the consequences of the pre-marital agreement and understood its impact throughout the marriage. The court determined that the pre-nuptial agreement was valid and the award was broadly in line with the husband's open offer.

Some elements of the husband's business proved difficult to value, partly due to the existence of a trust structure. Shares were held in private companies and he was not himself a shareholder. Four experts had been instructed and an exorbitant amount in costs had been expended by the parties on valuation evidence. Singer J found it would be disproportionate to seek further valuations of those interests, particularly given the complexities of the business structure, and felt unable to ascribe a value to those interests or to the likely future liquidity. The court, instead, used a broad-brush (or 'impressionistic') approach to ascertain the extent of the non-matrimonial property.

In order to make a fair distribution of the non-matrimonial assets, the judge made a '*Wells*' order[2], which provided the wife with shares in the husband's company. Absent a business valuation, the court held this was the fairest way to apportion risk.

At trial, the husband's open position had moved away from the agreement and reflected an element of sharing, such that the wife should receive £38 million of the capital assets and a 23.41% shareholding. The

[2] *Wells v Wells* [2002] EWCA Civ 476

wife's open proposal was that the capital should be divided so that she should receive £116 million (42.5%) and £157 million (57.5%) to the husband, to acknowledge the non-matrimonial nature of some of the assets.[3]

The wife was awarded half of the non-business assets (£51.4 million) and the *Wells* order amounted to a minority shareholding of 23.41% of the husband's business assets. This was a far better outcome for the wife than the approximately £27 million that would have been the case if the terms of the pre-marital agreement had been strictly applied.

It is noteworthy that the judge made it clear that the wife's behaviour and the court's unfavourable assessment of her credibility had no bearing on the award made to her; it did not amount to 'conduct it would be inequitable to disregard' and therefore this was not factored into the discretionary exercise.[4]

Appeal:

The wife appealed on four grounds: (i) the treatment of the pre-marital agreement; (ii) the treatment of non-matrimonial property; (iii) the failure to assess and place a value on the husband's business and the impact of this upon the sharing principle; and (iv) whether it was right to make a *Wells* order.

The wife's appeal failed, and the High Court decision was upheld by the Court of Appeal. Lady Justice King gave the leading judgment, alongside Lewison LJ and Holroyde LJ.

In respect of the first ground of appeal, the wife said that the pre-marital agreement should be ignored in its entirety, as the husband had departed from the terms of the pre-marital agreement, by putting forward an open position which was in line with the sharing principle. The wife stated

---

[3] *Versteegh v Versteegh, supra,* at [18] to [23]

[4] Section 25(2)(g), Matrimonial Causes Act 1973; *Versteegh* at [104]

that, as she did not have the benefit of legal advice, she did not have a full appreciation of the implications of the agreement. The court was not persuaded in respect of either of those points, confirming the wife had a full appreciation of the implications of the pre-marital agreement, despite the lack of legal advice (particularly given that pre-marital agreements are commonplace in Sweden), and it would not be right to add a gloss to the decision in *Radmacher*.[5]

The Court of Appeal further held that where there is a finding that a valid and effective pre-nuptial agreement exists, 'fairness' does not require a court to ignore the whole agreement just because one party chooses not to hold the other to its terms in its entirety. The husband's departure from the agreement in making a more generous offer did not, therefore, negate the agreement.

In respect of the second and third grounds, the Court of Appeal made it clear that there is no expectation upon a judge to take a detailed and arithmetic valuation to identify what constitutes non-matrimonial property; the assessment of non-matrimonial as against matrimonial assets is one part of the court's section 25 discretionary exercise. The Court of Appeal did, however, note that it is unusual to make no findings as to the valuation or liquidity.

The fourth ground of appeal also failed. The Court of Appeal held there are disadvantages to a *Wells* order, but it could cause unfairness to one or both parties if no attempt to share was made.

Lewison LJ helpfully set out that the key points from *Radmacher* are as follows:

[5] *Versteegh v Versteegh, supra,* at [65]

> "...i) Whether a [pre-nuptial agreement] is contractually binding or not is irrelevant. The court should apply the same principles whether or not a binding contract has been made: [63];
>
> ii) There is no need for black and white rules about the process leading up to the making of a [pre-nuptial agreement]. What matters is whether each party has all the information material to his or her decision, and that each should intend that the agreement should govern the financial consequences of the marriage coming to an end: [69];
>
> iii) Factors which would vitiate a contract will negate any effect that the [pre-nuptial agreement] might otherwise have had: [71]. But factors falling short of those which would vitiate a contract may reduce, rather than eliminate, the weight to be given to the [pre-nuptial agreement]: [72];
>
> iv) If the terms of the [pre-nuptial agreement] are unfair from the start this will reduce (not eliminate) the weight to be given to it: [73];
>
> v) If the parties to the [pre-nuptial agreement] are nationals of a state in which [pre-nuptial agreements] are common and binding, that will increase the weight to be given to the [pre-nuptial agreement]: [74];
>
> vi) In principle, if parties have made a [pre-nuptial agreement] there is no reason why they should not be entitled to enforce it: [52];
>
> vii) Thus, the court should give effect to a [pre-marital agreement] that is freely entered into by each party with a full appreciation of its implications unless in the circumstances prevailing it would not be fair to hold the parties to their agreement: [75];
>
> viii) Typically, it would not be fair to hold the parties to their agreement if it would prejudice the reasonable requirements of any children of the family [77]; or if holding them to the agreement would leave one spouse in a "predicament of real need": [81];
>
> ix) But in relation to the sharing principle the court is likely to make an order reflecting the terms of the [pre-marital agreement]: [82], [177] – [178]..."[6]

---

[6] *Versteegh v Versteegh, supra, per* Lewison LJ at [178]

Shortly after *Versteegh*, the Court of Appeal was tasked with determining a further appeal concerning pre-nuptial agreements.

Brack v Brack **[2018] EWCA Civ 2862** required the Court to consider three pre-nuptial agreements. The parties were Swedish nationals who had spent time living in the United States, Belgium and the United Kingdom, during their 14-year marriage. There were two children of the marriage. The husband had been a very successful racing driver, although his career was suddenly brought to an end as a result of a serious crash. The wife was a homemaker. The husband's substantial asset portfolio provided the parties' principal income after the accident. There were assets of around £11 million, £1.8 million of which represented the net equity in the family home.

The three pre-nuptial agreements had been created in the six months leading up to the marriage. They came to be known as: the 'Niagara agreement', the 'Ohio agreement' and the 'Gothenburg agreement'. The Niagara and Gothenburg agreements, created first and third in time, respectively, were said to have been made in identical terms. The Ohio agreement (entered into 18 days before marriage) was far more wide-ranging in its scope. The Ohio agreement contained a clause making it clear that a further agreement would be created within 90 days and specifically stated that where any "inconsistency, ambiguity or conflict"[7] existed between the Ohio agreement and the subsequent Gothenburg agreement, created three days before the marriage, the Gothenburg agreement should take precedence.

At first instance (Francis J):

The court held that all of the pre-nuptial agreements stated: (i) each party should retain their separate, individually acquired property (both pre and post marriage); (ii) that there should be no maintenance liability following separation; and, (iii) that the jurisdiction to resolve any issues following separation would be Stockholm, Sweden.

---

[7] *Brack v Brack, supra,* at [44], King LJ quoting words from the Ohio agreement

The court estimated that if the terms of the pre-nuptial agreements had been strictly adhered to, the wife would have been left with approximately five or six per cent of the asset base,[8] and this would have been manifestly unfair to the wife. The judge considered that, absent the pre-nuptial agreements and ensuing arguments about the terms and the issue of jurisdiction in respect of the maintenance prorogation clause, this was a case where the assets would have been "...broadly shared between the parties..."[9]

In deciding what award to make to the wife, the court first had to determine whether there was a valid prorogation clause, so as to decide whether the court's jurisdiction was constrained and, if so, to what extent. The judge's decision was informed by the requisite consideration of Article 4 of the Maintenance Regulation of Council Regulation (EC) No 4/2009 ('the Maintenance Regulation').

For a prorogation clause to be valid, Article 4 of the Maintenance Regulation requires the parties to have (a) made an agreement, which is (b) in writing. As both criteria were present, the court held that there was a valid prorogation clause, which effectively gave exclusive jurisdiction to the Swedish courts in respect of the parties' maintenance obligations. This purported to include jurisdiction on all 'needs', including housing.

Having decided the prorogation clause conferred jurisdiction in Sweden, the judge considered he was unable to make any orders under the Matrimonial Causes Act 1973. The judge did, however, decide that he retained jurisdiction to determine the parties' 'rights in property arising out of a matrimonial relationship' and, in an attempt to circumvent the "unfair" terms of the pre-nuptial agreements, made orders under the Married Women's Property Act 1882 and Schedule 1 to the Children Act 1989 so as to ensure the wife's needs were met.

---

[8] *Brack v Brack, supra,* at [23]

[9] *Brack v Brack* [2018] EWCA Civ 2862 at [12]

In finding that there was a valid pre-nuptial agreement the judge held, on the basis of established authorities post-*Radmacher*,[10] that he was constrained to make an award only on a 'needs' basis (to the extent that he was prohibited from applying the sharing or compensation principles).

Appeal:

The wife appealed on two grounds. The first ground was that the judge was wrong to state that, following a finding that a valid pre-nuptial agreement was unfair, he was restricted to making an award to the wife which was limited to her needs. The second ground was that there was no valid prorogation clause.

The Court of Appeal (as did Francis J) considered the question of the validity of the maintenance prorogation clause to be the logical first step to inform the subsequent issue of the court's assessment of the award, stating that "...absent the [maintenance prorogation clause], the case reverts to being a conventional financial remedies case..."[11]

The Court of Appeal disagreed with the judge's assessment of the three pre-nuptial agreements. Lady Justice King, giving the leading judgment, pointed out that agreed expert evidence confirmed that neither of the Niagara nor the Gothenburg agreements were enforceable in Sweden, both in respect of the prorogation clauses and the pre-nuptial agreement elements.[12] As such, neither of those agreements could be said to have contained valid prorogation clauses. By the time of the appeal, both parties were in agreement that if a valid maintenance prorogation clause were to exist, it could only be found within the Ohio agreement.

King LJ considered that "...prorogation clauses are very straightforward and require no complex drafting..."[13] and found that, although the Ohio

---

10 *Z v Z* [2011] EWHC 2878 and *Luckwell v Limata* [2014] EWHC 502

11 *Brack v Brack, supra,* at [40]

12 *Brack v Brack, supra,* at [41]

13 *Brack v Brack, supra,* at [58]

agreement was in writing, it did not automatically follow that the requirements of Article 4 of the Maintenance Regulation were met. The prorogation clause in the Ohio agreement made no reference to maintenance and the court found it could only be inferred by considering the rest of the pre-nuptial terms.

It was held that as the critical wording needed to be read from another part of the Ohio agreement, dealing with rights and not jurisdiction, this created an incomplete or unclear prorogation clause. The Court of Appeal applied the case of *Estasis Salotti di Colzani v Rüwa*[14] to the prorogation clause in the Ohio agreement.[15] As such, notwithstanding that the agreement was in writing and signed by the parties, the requirements of Article 4 were not fulfilled and the prorogation clause was held to be invalid.

King LJ further found even if the clause was capable of being valid, it would not have been because the Ohio agreement expressly stated that the Gothenburg agreement would take precedence over any "inconsistency, ambiguity or conflict". [16] There was no valid prorogation clause (since no valid clause appeared in the Gothenburg agreement). Lady Justice King cautioned:

> "...Failure to express a choice of jurisdiction in unambiguous terms can result, as here, in international jurisdictional disarray leading to delay and lengthy, complex litigation at extortionate cost."[17]

The Court of Appeal then turned to consider the wife's first ground of appeal. This was to determine whether, once there is a finding that there is a valid pre-nuptial agreement, the court should be restricted to making

[14] *Estasis Salotti di Colzani v Rüwa* [1976] ECR 1831

[15] *Estasis* involved Article 17 of the 1968 Brussels Convention, which is now superseded by Article 4 of the Maintenance Regulation

[16] *Brack v Brack, supra,* at [68]

[17] *Brack v Brack, supra,* at [75]

only a needs-based award. King LJ stated, "the judge [at first instance]… believed that so far as the pre-nuptial agreements were concerned… he was deprived of the ability to make any order which went beyond provision for the needs of the wife."[18]

By the time of appeal, it was stated to be "…common ground that in financial remedy proceedings, where a judge has found no vitiating features in relation to a pre-nuptial agreement, he is entitled, when applying the section 25 factors in his search for a fair outcome, to take into account needs, compensation and sharing. In other words, the fact of a valid pre-nuptial agreement does not necessarily (but may) lead inexorably to a solely needs-based outcome."[19]

The issue for the Court of Appeal was not to determine the extent of the wife's claims, as these would be remitted to the High Court. However, the Court of Appeal held that Francis J's conclusion based on the case law and the subsequent way in which the judge had directed himself was wrong. King LJ set out that a pre-nuptial agreement is just one of the factors to be considered within its discretionary statutory exercise and, as a matter of law, the court is not prevented from applying the sharing principle:

> "In the ordinary course of events, where there is a valid prenuptial agreement, the terms of which amount to [one party] having contracted out of a division of the assets based on sharing, a court is likely to regard fairness as demanding that [that party] receives a settlement that is limited to that which provides for [that party's] needs. But whilst such an outcome may be considered to be more likely than not, that does not prescribe the outcome in every case. Even where there is an effective prenuptial agreement, the court remains under an obligation to take into account all the factors found in s25(2) MCA 1973, together with a proper consideration of all of the circumstances, the first consideration being the welfare

[18] *Brack v Brack, supra,* at [37]

[19] *Brack v Brack, supra,* at [78] (*emphasis added*)

> of any children. Such an approach may, albeit unusually, lead the court in its search for a fair outcome, to make an order which, contrary to the terms of an agreement, provides a settlement for the [party] in excess of [the party's] needs."[20]

The case was remitted to the High Court for further consideration of the wife's claim. King LJ made it clear that the Court was not advocating that the lower court should make an award in excess of needs (that was a matter for the lower court), just that, as a matter of law, it was not prevented from doing so.

As a subscript, the litigation continued in the High Court.[21] In 2019, the wife applied to Francis J to set aside part of his judgment of 2016, namely that there were no vitiating factors present at the time the parties entered the three pre-nuptial agreements. The hearing was conducted remotely in May 2020, which Francis J reported he found to be of immense value, as he was able to replay the entire hearing.[22]

The wife lodged her application on the basis of 'new' evidence, which had been discovered by her only four days after the 2016 hearing and before judgment had been handed down. The 'new' evidence was email correspondence between the parties, written at the height of litigation in 2015. There was an argument about their admissibility, as the husband stated they attracted without prejudice privilege. It materialised that the evidence had clearly been contemplated by the wife in preparation for the proceedings, as a statement that was signed but not served was produced and the wife had (in the later statement that formed part of the proceedings) removed any reference to the email communications.

The judge found that there were three unexplainable periods of delay for the wife, with particular emphasis on the passage of three years post-trial, where the wife had failed to adduce the 'new' evidence. However, the

---

[20] *Brack v Brack* [2018] EWCA Civ 2862

[21] *Brack v Brack* [2020] EWHC 2142

[22] *Brack v Brack* [2020], *supra, per* Francis J at [3]

most critical assessment of the wife's conduct came against the backdrop of her having already had a determination on the issue of adducing 'new' evidence in the Court of Appeal. The wife's permission application in respect of the 'new' evidence had been "robustly turned down".[23] Accordingly, the judge struck out the wife's application, having determined it to be 'fatally flawed'. Francis J went on to say that even if he were able to admit the evidence, he would "...decisively exercise [his] discretion against the admission of the material, given the delay between the 'discovery' of the material... and [the wife's] attempt to introduce it..."[24]

Permission to Appeal Applications

Whilst all substantive judgments of the Court of Appeal are published, judgments on permission applications are only published if a judge so requests. The following post-*Radmacher* permission application judgments highlight the Court of Appeal's further treatment of pre-nuptial agreements.

The case of ***Luppi v Revesz* [2013] EWCA Civ 736** involved a pre-nuptial agreement that provided for each party to retain what they brought into the marriage and thereafter all assets to be shared. The agreement was signed nine days before the marriage in Venezuela, where they were living at the time. Three years afterwards, the parties moved to the United Kingdom. They separated after 15 years and there were two children of the marriage.

At trial, the judge made an award placing the "overwhelming emphasis on the needs of the children and for them to be housed"[25], including within the assets up for division a Venezuelan property that would otherwise be ringfenced. The wife received approximately 60 per cent of

[23] *Brack v Brack* [2020], *supra,* at [34]

[24] *Brack v Brack* [2020], *supra,* at [37]

[25] *Luppi v Revesz* [2013] EWCA Civ 736, *per* Vos LJ at [5]

the capital assets and the husband 40 per cent. It was also considered relevant, by the judge at first instance, His Honour Judge O'Dwyer, that the husband had an earning capacity but had chosen not to work. The latter point did not form part of the Court of Appeal's determination in the permission application. The husband appealed.

The appellant appeared in person, seeking permission to appeal in respect of eleven grounds, including: the judge took into account property he should not have (i.e. non-matrimonial property) and did not consider factors he ought to have done (including the possibility of insolvency in Venezuela); that he made the wrong award overall; that the judge had 'pierced the corporate veil' in respect of a Venezuelan company; and that there was incomplete disclosure by the wife. The appellant husband claimed that there was a *Barder*[26] event and that the judge was biased against him throughout proceedings. The appellant also sought to rely on rights conferred upon him under the European Convention on Human Rights to peaceful enjoyment of his possessions[27], to a fair trial[28] and the right to the enjoyment of his rights and freedoms secured without discrimination.[29]

Vos LJ, considering the permission application, stated: "…I have absolutely no doubt that an appeal in relation to those findings has no real prospect of success…"[30] The husband's application for permission to appeal was, therefore, dismissed.

The Court of Appeal confirmed, as stated in *Radmacher*, that children must not be prejudiced by the terms of a pre-nuptial agreement. The court's first consideration, in exercising its discretion, is always the minor children of a family. It was held that the first instance judge had properly considered the agreement to be unfair as it did not suitably provide for

---

[26] *Barder v Calouri* [1988] AC 20

[27] Article 1, Protocol 1, European Convention on Human Rights

[28] Article 6, European Convention on Human Rights

[29] Article 14, European Convention on Human Rights

[30] *Luppi v Revesz* [2013] EWCA Civ 1756, at [29]

the children of the family. The judge was found to be correct to depart from the parties' agreement as far as was necessary to ensure the children's needs for a home were met, by bringing into the matrimonial 'pot' a Venezuelan property that would otherwise have remained the sole, non-matrimonial, property of the husband.

The judgment of the McFarlane LJ in the permission application made in ***Currie v Monastyrski*** **[2017] EWCA Civ 1790** was also published by the Court of Appeal. Neither of the parties were on their first marriage and they had entered into a pre-nuptial agreement in which they agreed that each of their pre-acquired assets were to be ringfenced.

At first instance, the court held there was a valid pre-nuptial agreement. However, during the course of their marriage the parties mixed their assets to such an extent that the judge held that it would be unfair to hold the parties (in particular the husband) to the agreement. The court found as a fact that monies transferred by the husband to the wife from his re-mortgaging a solely-owned property had been used by the wife to invest in property in Dubai. It was the court's view that the actions of the parties demonstrated that their intentions had changed throughout the course of the marriage.

The court of first instance made an award that was "...a meticulously applied 50/50 division..."[31] of the assets. Within the judgment, Her Honour Judge Redgrave was very critical of the wife's credibility and "...concluded, it seems without any real doubt, that the wife was not being truthful."[32] Between the oral hearing and the handing down of judgment, the wife emailed the court with what was professed to be further 'material' evidence. The judge did not take this into consideration. There was no formal application to adduce further evidence and the husband, naturally, had no opportunity to consider the material or indeed make submissions.

[31] *Currie v Monastyrski* [2017] EWCA Civ 1790, *per* Sir Andrew McFarlane (as he now is) at [8]

[32] *Currie v Monastyrski, supra,* at [7]

The wife made an application for permission to appeal, which was first dealt with on the papers and refused. She resurrected her application, exercising her right to renew it at an oral hearing. It came before the Court of Appeal almost twelve months later. The appeal grounds were summarised, by McFarlane LJ as: (i) the judge's approach to the pre-nuptial agreement, (ii) the judge's approach to the wife's ownership of property and credibility (central to the appeal), and (iii) the way in which the judge exercised her discretion generally.[33]

The Court of Appeal upheld the decision of first instance and the wife's permission to appeal application was dismissed, it having been found to have "…no prospect of success at all".[34] The court held the judge's treatment of the pre-nuptial agreement to be unchallengeable: "… the process of dividing property at the end of a marriage is one in which the court has to take an overall view of the couple's finances and the way they have conducted themselves in a marriage, including the existence of any ante-nuptial agreement."[35]

The court expressed mild reservation in respect of one aspect of the wife's appeal, that being the judge's failure to take into account the further evidence that was emailed after the hearing but prior to judgment being handed down. However, the Court of Appeal considered the wife to have had ample opportunity to produce the so-called 'material' evidence at an earlier stage and deemed there was no error of law or principle on the judge's part in having adopted such a robust stance, particularly given the stage of proceedings in which it had been produced.

***

As evidenced by the above recent decisions, the Court will generally respect a party's autonomy and will hold the parties to a valid nuptial agreement, departing from it only as is necessary to meet needs. It is

---

33 *Currie v Monastyrski, supra,* at [15]

34 *Currie v Monastyrski, supra,* at [22]

35 *Currie v Monastyrski, supra,* at [17]

important to remember that a court is not precluded from making an award in excess of needs (albeit unusually). Conversely, parties should take care with property that is intended to be ringfenced. If there has been a degree of mixing of non-matrimonial assets the court may (depending on the extent) consider it to be unfair to hold the parties to a valid agreement if the parties' intentions appear to have changed.

CHAPTER SIX

COURTS IN RECENT YEARS II: THE HIGH COURT

This chapter sets out the High Court's approach to nuptial agreements over the last decade, after the Supreme Court's decision in *Radmacher v Granatino.*[1]

GS v L **[2011] EWHC 1759** (date of judgment 06.07.2011) appears to be the first reported case that applied the Supreme Court's decision in *Radmacher*. The case concerned two pre-marital agreements, signed in Spain, which had the effect of providing to the wife a 16.88 per cent share in the family home and thereafter all assets would be shared. Although there were assets of some £4 million, it was not a 'big money' case.[2]

Taking into account the circumstances existing at the time of their agreement, the court found that "...neither party had a full appreciation of the implications of the agreement..."[3], partly because the parties themselves were unsure of the precise terms and, perhaps more significantly, the Spanish legal experts appointed during the trial could not clarify the position in relation to Spanish law. The court held that once that finding was made, it was not necessary to go any further into an assessment of the fairness of the agreement.

Furthermore, the wife was reported to have felt financially vulnerable, and the husband confirmed in evidence that the motivation behind the agreement was not a potential divorce[4], but to protect the wife should

---

[1] *Radmacher v Granatino* [2010] UKSC 42

[2] *GS v L* [2011] EWHC 1759 at [3]

[3] *GS v L, supra, per* Eleanor King J at [79]

[4] *GS v L, supra, per* Eleanor King J at [77]

the husband pre-decease her. As such, it is questionable whether it amounted to a pre-nuptial agreement at all.

The issue of ringfencing was the subject of much legal debate. The court held that, ultimately, whilst the origin of assets was important it was necessary to invade the non-matrimonial assets to meet the needs of the wife and the children of the family.

Z v Z (Financial Remedy: Marriage Contract) [2011] EWHC 2878 involved French nationals, who married in France and who had lived there until they moved to England approximately one year before their separation. There were three minor children of the family. The parties had entered a pre-marital contract, electing the separation of property regime. The court held that, but for the pre-nuptial agreement, this would have been an equal sharing case. However, as the parties had clearly entered the agreement freely and with a full understanding of its implications (notwithstanding the absence of legal advice) the nuptial agreement was entirely valid. The pre-nuptial agreement was upheld by the court, in accordance with the Supreme Court's decision in *Radmacher*. It is of note that the court stated it would not have held the parties to the agreement if it had purported to exclude spousal maintenance.

Notably, the wife argued that the husband had made promises not to hold her to the pre-nuptial agreement. Moor J declined to decide whether it would be possible to vary a nuptial agreement orally but did consider the court would likely require the clearest possible evidence before even contemplating this.[5] The husband had written a letter to the wife offering to give her far more than would ever be awarded by a court; this offer was made without legal advice and at a time when the husband was in turmoil, during a trial separation, which the court held had fallen foul of the requirements of *Edgar*.[6] As such, the court held the letter did not

[5] *Z v Z (Financial Remedy: Marriage Contract)* [2011] EWHC 2878 *per* Moor J at [51-52]

[6] *Edgar v Edgar* [1980] 1 WLR 1410

provide a good reason for departing from the original pre-nuptial agreement.

The court upheld the pre-nuptial agreement (the first reported case to do so post the Supreme Court's decision) and the wife received 40 per cent of the assets, on a needs basis only, to account for the existence of a valid pre-nuptial agreement.

The case of ***V v V (Ancillary Relief: Pre-Nuptial Agreement)*** **[2011] EWHC 3230** concerned an Italian husband and a Swedish wife. The asset base was approximately £1.28 million, of which £1.15 million was in the husband's name. The parties had entered a pre-nuptial agreement, which stated that the husband's property was not to become 'marital property' and the marriage was contingent upon the parties entering the agreement. Notwithstanding that neither of the parties obtained independent legal advice, they were both found to have had a full appreciation of the terms and implications. However, the judge at first instance considered the agreement did no more than set out the property owned by the husband prior to the marriage, as it did not specify what the parties' entitlements should be upon divorce and decided that the agreement should be accorded little weight. The court held that the needs of the wife and the children required that the husband's pre-acquired property be included in the distribution and the family home was transferred to the wife, outright.

The husband appealed, stating that the district judge had erred in not giving sufficient weight to the pre-nuptial agreement. The husband argued that the family home should have been made subject to a charge, to recognise the existence of the agreement and reflect the agreement made.

The High Court allowed the husband's appeal, stating that once the court had made a finding that the parties had entered the agreement honestly, freely and knowingly the court should respect the parties' autonomous choice to have entered the agreement. The appellate court considered the judge had, in effect, adopted a pre-*Radmacher* approach. The court had failed to recognise the weight that should be attributed to the parties' autonomy.[7] Accordingly, the court made the property subject to a charge of 35.83 per cent in favour of the husband, which included the costs of the appeal, which the court found the wife should pay.

F v F (Financial Remedies: Premarital Wealth) **[2012] EWHC 438** involved parties who had entered post-nuptial settlements. There was some legal argument as to whether a share agreement was also a maintenance agreement. The family home was settled in a trust. The court held that the circumstances existing at the time of the divorce meant that the parties should not be held to their agreements, whether post-nuptial or maintenance agreements, and made a needs-based award.

Kremen v Agrest **[2012] EWHC 45** involved a very wealthy Russian couple who were embroiled in long-running, acrimonious litigation. The marriage was around 16 years, although there was a dispute about the validity of the marriage and, further, whether an earlier divorce had occurred. There were three children. At the time of the hearing, Mostyn J reported having given three previous judgments in the case and that by the time of his judgment in 2010, there had been no less than 50 orders made in respect of the parties.[8] Concurrently, there were proceedings variously in Russia and Israel concerning the validity of the parties' marriage.

The husband did not attend the hearing before Mostyn J, despite being specifically ordered to; notwithstanding this, the judge permitted the husband's MacKenzie friend to be in court and to lodge submissions on the husband's behalf, which were both scathing and abusive of the Court and the wife.[9] Two third parties had also intervened. One was seeking a charging order absolute and another "wide-ranging" application was before the court, which included a claim that the husband pay some £10 million in satisfaction of a debt. Both claims were dismissed, not least

---

[7] *V v V (Ancillary Relief: Pre-Nuptial Agreement)* [2011] EWHC 3230, *per* Charles J at [70]

[8] *Kremen v Agrest* [2012] EWHC 45, *per* Mostyn J at [15]

[9] *Kremen v Agrest, supra,* at [3]

because both had previously been determined and had been denied permission to appeal.[10]

The parties had entered a post-nuptial agreement during the marriage. It was created and signed in Israel (at some point, there was an apparent divorce in Israel, although the wife claimed to be unaware of this and the parties continued to live as husband and wife until separation). The wife had been advised by a 'relative' of the husband's. The agreement provided for the wife to receive approximately £1 million and to transfer any assets in her name to the husband.

At the time of the hearing, the husband claimed he was earning the equivalent of approximately £150 per month and had no assets; the wife alleged he had a net worth of at least £100 million. Against a background of a number of judicial findings that the husband was a "...serious and serial non-discloser... determined to do down his wife by 'foul means'..."[11], Mostyn J was completely satisfied that the husband had set out to actively mislead both the wife and the Court. The court found the husband to be motivated by a "...mixture of a wish selfishly to protect his fortune for himself, even at the expense of his children, and a desire to inflict the maximum economic harm to [the wife]..."[12]

The Court decided the post-nuptial agreement should be accorded no weight at all and discarded it from its discretionary assessment. Mostyn J had no hesitation in concluding the following:

> "...i) W did not freely enter into the agreement with a <u>full appreciation</u> of its implications. It was the product of pressure from H and there was a material absence of independent legal advice and disclosure.

---

[10] *Kremen v Agrest, supra,* at [81], [82]

[11] *Kremen v Agrest, supra,* at [35]

[12] *Kremen v Agrest, supra,* at [36]

> ii) Moreover, it is doubtful that the parties ever actually intended that the agreement should govern the financial consequences of the marriage coming to an end.
>
> iii) It would be grossly unfair to hold W to an agreement which deprived her of her fair share of a fortune to the formation of which she has, in her own way, equally contributed.
>
> iv) Moreover, the agreement did not then, nor does it now, remotely meet her reasonable needs.
>
> v) And the agreement grossly prejudices the needs of the children…"[13]

An award of £12.5 million was made to the wife, which included an equal share of the marital fortune to which she contributed and a needs-based award of £8.3 million, with the court certifying the award constituted 'maintenance'[14] pursuant to the EU Maintenance Regulation 4/2009 for the purposes of any enforcement proceedings the wife was required to initiate in another jurisdiction.

Within the judgment, Mostyn J considered it would be "…an unusual case where it can be said that absent independent legal advice and full disclosure, a party can be taken to have freely entered into a marital agreement with a <u>full appreciation</u> of its implications… and that "…it would surely have to be shown that the spouse, like Mr Granatino, had a high degree of financial and legal sophistication in order to have a full appreciation of what legal rights he or she is signing away…"[15] However, Mostyn J's strict interpretation would appear to be contrary to the Court

---

13 *Kremen v Agrest, supra, per* Mostyn J at [15]

14 Under the Maintenance Regulation, 'maintenance' extends to capital provision in other jurisdictions

15 *Kremen v Agrest, supra,* at [73]

of Appeal's approach in *Versteegh*[16] and *Brack*[17] and other High Court authorities because agreements have been upheld where no such 'high degree of financial and legal sophistication' is apparent.

In ***B v S (Financial Remedy: Marital Property)*** **[2012] EWHC 265**, the parties had created a pre-nuptial agreement in Catalonia, which, "almost uniquely"[18] has a 'separation of property' regime as default. The wife was Spanish and the husband of another nationality, which was referred to only as 'Country A' by the court, in order to preserve anonymity. The parties also entered into a post-nuptial separation of property agreement in Country A, in respect of specific property belonging to the wife so as to circumvent Country A's default 'community of property' regime.

Mostyn J considered there to be "…a marked difference between a negotiated pre-nuptial agreement which specifically contemplates divorce and which seeks to restrict or influence the exercise of discretion to which the law gives access, and an agreement made in a civil jurisdiction which adopts a particular marital property regime…"[19]. The court held that the only way that foreign law is relevant to the determination of the case (or any case involving a nuptial agreement) is in relation to the parties' intentions.[20]

The court held that neither party had a full appreciation of the implications of the pre-nuptial agreement, particularly with regard to its enforceability upon divorce in England or in the USA where they had previously lived. Neither party received advice as to the effect of the agreement on their rights were they to divorce in a jurisdiction of equitable jurisdiction. Further, the court held, *inter alia*, that the aim of the post-nuptial agreement was to protect specific property (rather than it being made in contemplation of divorce). It is important to note that

---

16 *Versteegh v Versteegh* [2018] EWCA Civ 1050

17 *Brack v Brack* [2018] EWCA Civ 2862

18 *B v S (Financial Remedy: Marital Property)* [2012] EWHC 265 at [4]

19 *B v S (Financial Remedy: Marital Property)* at [5]

20 *B v S (Financial Remedy: Marital Property)* at [10]

the Court of Appeal, in *Versteegh*, has since rejected the strict proposition that parties must have advice with regard to how the agreement would operate in a discretionary system in order to have had a full appreciation of its terms.[21]

AH v PH (Scandinavian Marriage Settlement) **[2013] EWHC 3873** concerned a Scandinavian couple who were living in England. They had signed a pre-marital agreement the day before the wedding (both having been advised by lawyers who practised in their country of origin), which identified the wife's housing need in Scandinavia and ringfenced the husband's inherited wealth. It did not become registered. The court found that the wife did not have a full appreciation of the implications. The pre-nuptial agreement was predicated on the wife living in Scandinavia and she did not have any understanding of the implications if she were to remain living in England; she was never advised to obtain legal advice in this jurisdiction and so was unaware of the discretionary approach to matrimonial finance on divorce. Further, the court found that, as the fact the authorities in Scandinavia failed to register the marital agreement, this would lead to the natural conclusion that it was not binding. Finally, the husband's admission that he knew the English courts were 'generous' to wives (but he did not share that information with the wife or seek to include reference to it in the pre-nuptial agreement) placed the parties on an unequal footing.

The court reinforced its decision to attribute no weight to the pre-nuptial agreement by noting that it would not be unjust to the husband. The court found: the wife's housing need was necessarily different, because the husband has requested the wife and children continue to reside in England; the husband had acted in a way that demonstrated he did not consider himself bound by the agreement, post separation; and the husband had promised the wife that he would provide generously for her in the event of a divorce. The court made a needs-based award, invading the husband's inheritance as far as was necessary to do so.

[21] See *Versteegh v Versteegh, supra, per* Lady Justice King at [182]

In *BN v MA (Maintenance Pending Suit: Pre-Nuptial Agreement)* **[2013] EWHC 4250**, the court determined the effect of a pre-nuptial agreement on the wife's applications for maintenance pending suit, interim periodical payments for children[22] and a legal services provision order. The pre-nuptial agreement had been negotiated over approximately two years, from the date of the parties' engagement. The agreement was considered to be "highly influential" by the court, in particular an 'important notice' on the fact of the nuptial agreement which made it clear the parties intended to: create contractual relations between the parties; confirm their separate property interests; that the agreement was to govern the parties' finances on divorce; and that they intended to be bound by its terms.[23]

The court held, "...when adjudicating a question of interim maintenance, where there has been a pre-nuptial agreement, the court should seek to apply the terms of the pre-nuptial agreement as closely and practically as it can, unless the evidence of the wife in support of her application demonstrates, to a convincing standard, that she has a prospect of satisfying a court that the agreement should not be upheld... provided that the wife is not left in any predicament of real need..."[24]

Accordingly, the court made an award for interim maintenance, assessed in accordance with the terms of the pre-nuptial agreement. The husband was given credit for other payments he was making. Periodical payments for the children could not be made as a separate order, as the court did not have jurisdiction to make the order applied for where the application stated the children were (or would be) habitually resident in England and Wales. The children's needs (that of the parties' 8-year-old and the child they were expecting) were encompassed within the court's assessment of the wife's needs and child maintenance provision made. The wife's application for a legal services provision order was refused because she

---

[22] Application made under section 23(1)(d) of the Matrimonial Causes Act 1973

[23] *BN v MA (Maintenance Pending Suit: Pre-Nuptial Agreement)* [2013] EWHC 4250 at [5]

[24] *BN v MA, supra,* at [33]

was unable to satisfy the court that she could not obtain a litigation loan (the court finding that she would reasonably be able to obtain legal advice without the allowance); *Currey v Currey*[25] applied. The wife's claims were found to be "extremely speculative" and "borderline irresponsible". She had not produced a sufficiently detailed schedule of legal costs and the court found that it would not have made a costs allowance in any event.[26]

SA v PA (Pre-Marital Agreement: Compensation) [2014] EWHC 392 concerned an English wife and a Dutch husband, with four children. The husband was described as "...a successful solicitor in a magic circle firm...".[27] Both parties were described as being "...highly intelligent people..."[28]
The capital assets amounted to approximately £3.8 million. The parties had entered a pre-nuptial agreement one day before the marriage, in Amsterdam. The agreement did not deal with maintenance and the court was free to make an award in that regard. Mostyn J made it clear that a valid pre-nuptial agreement could deal with some and not all classes of assets.[29]

The court held it was fair to implement the terms of the pre-nuptial agreement, as against the capital assets. Although the agreement was signed the day before the wedding, when the wife was pregnant and she only received impartial (and not independent) advice from the notary, the wife was found to have been privy to all the draft agreements. The wife was held to its terms, the court finding that she entered the agreement freely with an appreciation of its implications.[30] This was despite it being written in Dutch, as the wife had made extensive annotations on an early draft of the agreement in English and she had added some Dutch words to the declarations the parties were to sign. The

[25] *Currey v Currey* [2007] 1 FLR 946

[26] *Currey v Currey, supra,* at [38]

[27] *SA v PA, (Pre-Marital Agreement: Compensation)* [2014] EWHC 392 at [1]

[28] *SA v PA, supra,* at [39]

[29] *SA v PA, supra,* at [54]

[30] *SA v PA, supra,* at [63]

court also found that the parties had intended the agreement would be binding upon them in whichever jurisdiction they chose to divorce.[31] The court also made an award of spousal maintenance[32], capitalised as far as was possible with the husband being required to pay periodical payments in respect of the shortfall, over five years (with an extendable term).

The other significant factor in the case was the wife's claim for compensation, having given up her legal career to focus on the family. The court was not satisfied that the wife had met the high threshold for establishing compensation:[33]

> "...with all due respect, I totally disagree that this is a compensation case. The wife had no appreciable track record by the time she gave up work. It is not even known what she was earning when she quit, let alone whether they were high earnings. It is impossible to speculate where she would be now had she made different decisions at that time..."[34]

The case of ***Luckwell v Limata*** **[2014] EWHC 502** was (unusually) heard in public, pursuant to FPR 21.10(1)(b), the court having decided that the matter was of considerable and legitimate public interest and that there should be greater transparency in the family courts. It was an eight-year marriage and there were three children of the family. The case involved a pre-nuptial agreement and two post-nuptial agreements made in effectively the same terms: that the husband would not make any claim in relation to the wife's separate property or in respect of any gifts made to the wife by her wealthy family. The court was 'sure' that the marriage would not have taken place without the pre-nuptial agreement. There was a clause within the agreement to that effect and both parties expressly

[31] *SA v PA, supra,* at [60]

[32] The court's award was made on the basis of a Duxbury calculation based on a 54-year-old woman at £65,000 per annum: £1,281,000

[33] See chapter 2 for the legal principles applicable in compensation claims

[34] *SA v PA, supra,* at [68]

agreed, during their evidence, that this was an accurate reflection of the circumstances.[35] The court found that without the supplemental agreements, the substantial gifts would not have been made.[36]

Neither party had any significant income and the court remarked that at the end of proceedings, primarily as a result of the costs of litigation resulting in an "exceptionally bitter hearing"[37] the husband had no assets at all and although the wife owned, unencumbered, the £6.74 million property in which she lived; she had no other free assets. Both parties' liabilities exceeded their assets.

The wealth was with the wife's family and, whilst the wife's father had initially been willing to act as guarantor for the wife to obtain a mortgage in order to pay to the husband a lump sum, this had been rejected by the husband. The wife's primary open position at trial was said to be "…not to offer a penny…"[38]. The court appeared to express a degree of dismay that the parties had been unable to settle, and saw the case as one that was "eminently capable of settlement"[39].

The court held that the husband knew exactly what he was foregoing when he signed the three agreements over the course of 2 ½ years and he "…absolutely intended to be bound by them…". Holman J also confirmed that the husband could not establish any claim for sharing, contributions or compensation. Notwithstanding these findings, the court was compelled to make a needs-based award, with 'needs' being the only consideration capable of not holding the parties to their agreement absolutely.[40] The court accounted for the three children of the family being the court's first consideration and made an award to meet the husband's pressing need for secure accommodation for himself and the

---

35 *Luckwell v Limata* [2014] EWHC 502, *per* Holman J at [12]

36 *Luckwell v Limata, supra,* at [1]

37 *Luckwell v Limata, supra,* at [6]

38 *Luckwell v Limata, supra,* at [6]

39 *Luckwell v Limata, supra,* at [7]

40 *Luckwell v Limata, supra,* at [138]

children, ensuring the home for the father would not demean him as against the wife's standard of accommodation.

The husband was, effectively, awarded a life interest in a property. The wife was to produce a housing fund of £900,000 plus purchase costs and the court stated that property should be sold when the youngest child is 22 (notably the same age specified in *Radmacher*). Forty-five per cent of the net proceeds of sale would then revert to the wife and the remainder reinvested in a new, smaller property for the remainder of the husband's life. The wife was also ordered to pay a lump sum of £292,000 for the husband to furnish a property, buy a car and discharge his liabilities. Holman J stated that but for the nuptial agreements, he would have made the housing award outright to the husband.

Y v Y (Financial Remedy: Marriage Contract) [2014] EWHC 2920 involved French nationals, living in France at the time of their marriage, who moved to London shortly after the birth of their first child. They had been living in England for the majority of their 22-year marriage (to the date of decree nisi, some years before the trial). Roberts J held that the parties' place of domicile continued to be in France due to their substantial connections there, including property investments, family and social ties and the children having each received a French education. The parties had entered into a pre-marital contract electing the separation of property regime, which would be absolutely binding on the parties in France.[41] The asset base was around £13 million, of which £1 million was said to be pre-marital. Under the terms of the nuptial agreement, the parties would retain their individual pre-acquired and post-marriage assets.

Roberts J made numerous findings in respect of the pre-nuptial agreement[42], including that both parties were very busy in the lead up to the wedding and working long hours. The wife was fully engaged in wedding planning and was also pregnant. The court found that the wife

[41] *Y v Y (Financial Remedy: Marriage Contract)* [2014] EWHC 2920 at [5]

[42] *Y v Y, supra,* at [67]

understood the pre-marital contract was intended to govern the parties' finances during the marriage but that she did not have "...a full appreciation and understanding of its intended effect on death or divorce..."[43] at the date of marriage. It was found that the wife did not have all of the information material to her decision to enter the nuptial agreement or that she intended it to govern their financial consequences in the event of a divorce.[44]

However, the court was clear that a finding that there was a lack of understanding in relation to a pre-nuptial agreement does not mean that it automatically falls away, it is a matter of the degree of weight that should be attributed.[45] Roberts J determined that, in this scenario, the existence of the pre-nuptial agreement will still be one of the circumstances of the case.[46]

Agreeing with Mostyn J, in *B v S*,[47] Roberts J held that, "...the parties must have intended the agreement to apply wherever they might be divorced and, in particular, if they were divorced in a regime that operated a system of discretionary equitable distribution..."[48] and considered it would be wise for the other party's legal adviser to insert a clause dealing with this. However, the court made it clear that advice from every possible jurisdiction would not be required, stating, "...that does not mean that parties will need to seek advice on all possible permutations; such a result would be plainly absurd."[49]

In light of the above findings, the court decided that the husband had not made out his case in relation to the enforceability of the pre-marital contract in its strict terms. This was because it was "impossible" to say

43 Y v Y, *supra,* at [67(xiv)]

44 *Y v Y, supra,* at [109]

45 *Y v Y, supra,* at [69]

46 *Y v Y, supra,* at [68]

47 *B v S (Financial Remedy: Marital Property)* [2012] EWHC 265

48 *Y v Y, supra,* at [53]

49 *Y v Y, supra,* at [110]

that the wife had all information material to her decision and/or that the wife intended the agreement to govern the parties' finances on divorce.[50] Neither party was seeking a share of the other's pre-acquired property and so that would be ringfenced, subject to the wife's needs. The marital acquest would be shared, broadly equally.[51] The award made represented a small departure from equality of division in respect of the marital acquest, to reflect the wife's onshore cash reserves, which were greater than the husband's, and for likely tax efficiency.

In ***L v M*** **[2014] EWHC 2220**, the principles of *Radmacher* were applied in respect of a separation agreement. The parties were both British but had strong connections to Africa. The family home was in Zimbabwe and they had a holiday home in Kenya. The wife had made an application for notice to show cause as to why the husband should not be held to the terms of a separation agreement, which had been made into a draft (but signed) consent order. The husband (found to have a worth amounting to many millions of pounds[52]) had acted upon the agreement, by paying part of a lump sum but later resiled upon it claiming, *inter alia*, that there was insufficient disclosure and that he did not receive any legal advice. Although initially represented, by the time of the hearing the husband was not represented and he did not attend court. Nonetheless, the judge undertook a full investigation of the circumstances of the case and made a determination.

The agreement made it clear that the parties had not provided financial disclosure to each other, but that they had a sufficient understanding so that the provision made for the wife and child was 'reasonable' provision. The agreement also stated that the parties had taken, or had the opportunity to obtain, legal advice.

The court held the husband to the agreement, subject to some minor concessions by the wife, considering him to have had ample opportunity

---

[50] *Y v Y, supra,* at [109]

[51] *Y v Y, supra,* at [111]

[52] *L v M* [2014] EWHC 2220 at [78]

to have sought legal advice on the agreement, and, in any event, found it was freely entered into by the husband, with a full appreciation of the implications.[53]

Hopkins v Hopkins **[2015] EWHC 812** concerns a post-nuptial agreement, entered into four months after the marriage, and an application by the husband for a notice to show cause as to why the wife should not be held to the terms of the agreement. The parties had a complex relationship history going back over approximately four decades, although the marriage itself was only three years. Notably, the agreement was entered into approximately five months after the 'landmark' decision in *Radmacher*.[54]

The wife argued the agreement should not be upheld because it was "…vitiated by duress; alternatively unconscionable conduct such as undue pressure (falling short of duress); alternatively other unworthy conduct, such as exploitation of a dominant position to secure an unfair advantage…"[55] The wife asked the court to take into account her emotional state at the time of the agreement.

The wife had received clear and repeated advice not to enter the nuptial agreement. The court held that it was very relevant that the terms of the agreement as they had evolved were generally based upon the express requests of the wife.[56] Ultimately, the court found the agreement was freely entered into by both parties with full advice and it was an agreement that paid due regard to the wife's needs.[57] It was fair to hold the parties to their agreement and it would have been unfair to the husband to make any different order for financial provision.[58]

---

[53] *L v M, supra,* at [71]

[54] *Hopkins v Hopkins* [2015] EWHC 812 at [2]

[55] *Hopkins v Hopkins, supra,* at [2]

[56] *Hopkins v Hopkins, supra,* at [79]

[57] *Hopkins v Hopkins, supra,* at [88]

[58] *Hopkins v Hopkins, supra,* at [90]

In *Gray v Work* [2015] **EWHC 834** the parties, both American and living in England, had signed two post-nuptial agreements (one signed immediately after the other) around five years into their long marriage of approximately 20 years. The husband earned considerable wealth of some £144 million, entirely during the marriage and mainly over the course of eight years when the parties lived in Japan. If the terms of the post-nuptial agreements were to be strictly applied, the husband would be left with approximately 98 per cent of the wealth, and the wife just two per cent. The court gave great encouragement to the parties to settle throughout the proceedings but this was plainly not possible and the court described the hearing as "…one of unedifying and destructive pugilism…"[59]

The post-nuptial agreements had been created and signed in Texas, although the parties' only link to Texas was that was where the headquarters of the company the husband worked for was located. The court found that the main purpose of the agreement was to partition the parties' separate property in anticipation of the husband's expatriation, which he was doing for tax efficiency reasons. The wife said she understood the separation of property agreement had to be 'watertight' so that the American tax authorities could not pursue the wealth via her status, as spouse and citizen of America. The wife also relinquished her American citizenship, but not until 14 years later.[60]

The court held the nuptial agreements to be of no relevance to and would have no impact upon the proceedings in England. There was no jurisdiction clause electing the law of Texas and it was therefore found that the discretionary approach in England and Wales should apply.[61] Holman J further held that if the court was wrong in that determination, applying *Radmacher*, the circumstances attending to the creation of the agreement made it so that the wife "most certainly"[62] could not be said

---

[59] *Gray v Work* [2015] EWHC 834, *per* Holman J at [6]

[60] *Gray v Work, supra* at [41]

[61] *Gray v Work, supra,* at [95 – 97]

[62] *Gray v Work, supra,* at [99]

to have had a full appreciation of the implications of the terms. As such, in any event, the agreements would be accorded no weight or effect.

The court carried out its discretionary exercise and Holman J stated that fairness would be achieved by making an award for an equal division of the parties' assets.[63] The court rejected the husband's claim that he had made a special contribution.

Incidentally, the husband appealed to the Court of Appeal[64], but not in respect of the court's decision regarding the nuptial agreement. The husband's appeal was based on his unmatched special contribution, which he argued should have led to the court making an award that was a departure from equality. The husband's appeal was dismissed. The Court of Appeal upheld the decision of Holman J, finding that the correct approach to assessing special contribution had been taken.

The case of ***WW v HW (Pre-Nuptial Agreement: Needs: Conduct)* [2015] EWHC 1844** involved parties who had signed a pre-nuptial agreement three weeks before their wedding. The primary aim of the agreement was to protect the wife's interest in a family trust worth £27 million, which had been inherited from her father. The judge considered that the high expenditure on legal costs (circa £1.77 million) made it a "…paradigm example of a case which demonstrates the need for more certainty in the law of financial remedies and nuptial agreements…"[65]

The court generally preferred the wife's evidence, although made criticism of both parties for feigning forgetfulness, at times, during cross-examination.[66] The husband was found to have deliberately misled the wife and her legal advisers as to the extent of his income prior to the marriage; he presented himself as someone with a lucrative career, who

63 *Gray v Work, supra,* at [160]

64 *Work v Gray* [2017] EWCA Civ 270

65 *WW v HW (Pre-Nuptial Agreement: Needs: Conduct)* [2015] EWHC 1844, *per* Mr Cusworth QC, at [1]

66 *WW v HW, supra,* at [11]

would not be dependent upon his (then) wife-to-be. The court determined that the husband's motive for the "substantial exaggeration" was probably to reassure the wife that he was not entering the marriage for financial reasons,[67] although he continued to maintain that he enjoyed a very profitable pre-marriage income (which was not the case) until around six months before the trial. The husband was also found to have deliberately and unfairly passed a tax liability on to the wife.[68]

The court held that the nuptial agreement should be accorded significant weight: "...Both parties understood the agreement, had the opportunity for full advice about its contents, entered into it freely and intended that it should be binding upon them at the point when it was executed. Both parties were comparatively mature, and neither sought to exploit a dominant position..."[69] It was fair to hold the husband to the agreement and it would have been unfair to the wife not to do so.

The court considered the husband's conduct had "...infected the course of [the] litigation..." and held that in circumstances where the biggest risk to the husband's future financial security was uncertainty related to tax penalties (created by the conduct of the husband) the court did not need to be "overly protective" of the husband when assessing his needs.[70] Accordingly, the court made a needs-based award to the husband (£1.7 million for housing), primarily to account for his role as a father with a step-down in accommodation when the youngest child is 23 with 45 per cent of the housing fund reverting to the wife. In deeming the reversionary interest to be fair, the court factored in not only the costs of the financial remedy proceedings but the very significant costs incurred by the wife in respect of HMRC proceedings.[71]

---

67 *WW v HW, supra,* at [16]

68 *WW v HW, supra,* at [59]

69 *WW v HW, supra,* at [50]

70 *WW v HW, supra,* at [64]

71 *WW v HW, supra* at [74]

In ***Joy v Joy-Morancho* [2015] EWHC 2507**, it was argued that a trust settlement was a post-nuptial agreement; however, the court held it had not been established in contemplation of marriage. The husband was found to have displayed "blatant dishonesty"[72] regarding his financial position (he and the trustee were found to have presented an "elaborate charade"[73] about the husband's future access to trust funds). As a result of the court's finding that there had been such a gross false presentation of assets[74] the wife was awarded periodical payments only, with an adjournment of her outstanding capital claims.[75] The court expressed a degree of reluctance in not achieving finality in litigation but held that this was a case where "…fairness and justice must prevail…".[76]

***Mantegazza v Mantegazza* [2017] EWHC 3811** concerned an English wife and a Swiss husband. The parties had married in Switzerland and had signed a pre-nuptial agreement, on the day of the wedding, electing the Swiss separation of property regime. The agreement stated that jurisdiction would lay with Switzerland in the event of divorce.

The parties lived in England for the early years of their marriage and then moved to Switzerland for the last 11 years of marriage, where they remained living until separation. The wife issued proceedings in England and Wales, on the basis of her domicile. The husband issued in Switzerland, where proceedings were stayed pending the outcome of the wife's application. The court in England and Wales required the husband to prove that Switzerland was the appropriate forum, which the court determined it was for several reasons.[77] Once the husband had established this, the wife then had to show that she would not obtain substantial justice in Switzerland.[78] The court came to the clear conclusion that the

---

[72] *Joy v Joy-Morancho* [2015] EWHC 2507, *per* Sir Peter Singer, at [210]

[73] *Joy v Joy-Morancho, supra,* at [170]

[74] *Joy v Joy-Morancho, supra,* at [221]

[75] *Joy v Joy-Morancho, supra,* at [175]

[76] *Joy v Joy-Morancho, supra,* at [176]

[77] *Mantegazza v Mantegazza* [2017] EWHC 3811, *per* Moor J at [49]

[78] *Mantegazza v Mantegazza, supra,* at [33]

wife was unable to show this and Moor J remitted the case to Switzerland for final determination.[79]

The parties in the case of ***KA v MA (Pre-Nuptial Agreement: Needs)* [2018] EWHC 499** were both on second marriages. The husband was an affluent businessman and the wife was a homemaker. There were assets of £23 million – £33 million. The husband had three children from his first marriage and had been through a very protracted divorce from his first wife. He was said to be very reluctant to marry for a second time. The parties had cohabited for several years, and the wife had been akin to a stepmother to the husband's children well before the marriage. The parties had a son, aged 4 at the time of the marriage.

The wife held a strong belief in marriage and had always made it clear that she wanted to marry in the longer term. Shortly after the birth of their child, the wife began to press the husband to marry. One key aspect of the wife's desire to marry becoming more pressing was that she did not want the child to have a different surname. Conversely, the husband had always made it clear to the wife that, whilst he was absolutely committed to her, he resolutely did not want to marry because of the profoundly difficult divorce he had been through. The husband suggested the wife change her name by deed poll, but she did not agree. The parties agreed to marry but the husband made it clear that it would be on the condition that there was a pre-nuptial agreement. The wife's evidence was that the parties had an 'understanding' that there would be no marriage without a nuptial agreement.[80]

The parties entered a pre-nuptial agreement, which would have provided the wife with £1.6 million. The wife made a needs-based claim of £6 million and the husband applied for a notice to show cause as to why the wife should not be held to the terms of the agreement.

[79] *Mantegazza v Mantegazza, supra,* at [63]

[80] *KA v MA (Pre-Nuptial Agreement: Needs)* [2018] EWHC 499, at [7]

The wife argued that she had been pressured into signing the agreement and had either been subjected to duress or the husband had exploited a dominant position, by his taking the stance that no marriage would take place but for the pre-nuptial agreement. The wife asked the court to take into account her emotional state at the time of signing. The agreement was signed a short time after an argument between the parties about the terms.

Both parties waived legal professional privilege, so that Roberts J was able to analyse the advice given to the parties. The wife had entered the agreement notwithstanding that her solicitor advised her not to sign as she would be "substantially better off" if she did not sign.[81] The court also had sight of an attendance note that the wife was very distressed and that there had been an altercation between the parties. There were two further attendance notes that were relevant: firstly, that the wife was calmer but would like to consider her position on the agreement overnight and, secondly, the following day, that she was content for the signed pre-nuptial agreement to be sent to the husband's solicitors.

The court was satisfied that the wife fully understood the terms of the agreement and that she intended to be bound by those terms. It was determined that the wife knew from the advice she received that the agreement would leave her worse off than would otherwise be the case, if the section 25 factors were applied absent the agreement.[82] Having found that a valid nuptial agreement existed, and it was fair to hold the parties to their agreement, Roberts J made a needs-based award to the wife of £2.73 million, taking particular account of the court's first regard being the welfare of the parties' child.[83]

Ipekçi v McConnell **[2019] EWFC 19** concerned a pre-nuptial agreement entered into by an American wife and a husband of Turkish heritage, who met in New York. It was an 11-year marriage with two

[81] *KA v MA, supra,* at [39]

[82] *KA v MA, supra,* at [46]

[83] *KA v MA, supra,* at [90] and [136]

children. The wife was a wealthy heiress (the great-granddaughter of the creator of Avon and a beneficiary of trusts worth approximately $65 million). The husband was a hotel concierge and he owned capital assets worth around £50,000, which included an interest in his mother's home in Turkey. The parties signed the pre-nuptial agreement 15 days before the wedding, which provided for a separation of property. There were two children of the family.

Mostyn J had no hesitation in deciding that it would be wholly unfair to hold the husband to the pre-nuptial agreement in the circumstances surrounding the creation of the agreement.[84] The agreement purported to be governed by New York law; however, expert evidence confirmed that the absence of a duly authenticated certificate meant that, in New York, the agreement would be accorded 'minimal weight, if any'. Also, the husband received legal advice from a lawyer who had no expertise in New York law, which, the court held, meant that he could not be said to have had a full appreciation of the implications of the agreement. Furthermore, the court held the fact the solicitor advising the husband had acted for the wife in her previous divorce gave rise to a situation where there was a clearly a situation of apparent bias. Finally, the husband would have been left in a predicament of real need.

The court rejected the evidence of a trustee which was received extremely late (by letters, addressed to Mostyn J received during the trial itself) and which the court found contradicted the trust documentation. The court held that the trustee's evidence was factual and not expert evidence and stated that even if it were correct, it would have been accorded no weight on the basis that it was received so late and because there was no opportunity for the husband to cross-examine the trustee or obtain his own evidence.[85] The wife was found to be the sole beneficiary of a discretionary trust and was found to have the trust funds available to her for satisfying the court's judgment.[86]

---

[84] *Ipekçi v McConnell* [2019] EWFC 19 at [27]

[85] *Ipekçi v McConnell, supra,* at [11]

[86] *Ipekçi v McConnell, supra,* at [12]

As all the assets (on both sides) were non-matrimonial in origin, the court made a needs-based award of £1.33 million, factoring in the husband's housing needs (£750,000, subject to a charge back to the wife of £375,000 repayable on the death of the husband, either to the wife or her estate), liabilities (including legal fees) and a Duxbury fund of capitalised maintenance.[87] The award was made on a clean break basis and the court decreed an indemnity in the husband's favour in case the wife made a claim for child maintenance under the Child Support Act 1991.

The parties' solicitors were heavily criticised for their non-compliance with FPR PD27A (relating to bundles) and the Efficiency Statement of 1 February 2016.[88] The one bundle rule had been exceeded, without permission. There were many duplicated and irrelevant documents, whilst relevant documents had been omitted. The parties had made no attempt to agree preliminary documents and a late delivery of bundles impacted on the late filing of skeleton arguments. Mostyn J expressed "great disquiet and dismay" and cautioned the legal advisers that to "...ensure that in no case in the future does such non-compliance recur..."[89]

The case of ***MT v VA (Second Application: Legal Services Provision Order)* [2020] EWHC 3087** was an application by the husband for a legal services provision order (LSPO) so that he could clear outstanding legal fees (due in part to the wife's appeal of the husband's previous application for a LSPO) and obtain legal advice. There was a pre-nuptial agreement, which the husband said ought to be considered by the court in light of his contributions to the marriage. The terms of the pre-nuptial agreement provided that the husband would not make a claim against the wife's non-matrimonial assets. As this was an interim hearing in respect of the application for a LSPO, the issues for determination

[87] *Ipekçi v McConnell, supra,* at [34]

[88] Statement on the Efficient Conduct of Financial Remedy Hearings Allocated to a High Court Judge, 2016, Mostyn J, 1 February 2016

[89] *Ipekçi v McConnell, supra,* at [39]

remained, including the circumstances existing at the time of the agreement and untested allegations of non-disclosure by the wife. Roberts J made a legal services provision order of £95,000 (without prejudice to either party inviting the court to make a costs order at the conclusion of financial proceedings).[90]

The case of ***AD v BD* [2020] EWHC 857** concerned a pre-nuptial agreement that had been signed the day before the marriage ceremony, in France (at the Embassy of 'Country A'). The wife was a French and 'Country A' national. The husband was a national of France, Canada and 'Country A'. There were two children of the marriage. The parties both came from wealthy families and around three years before separation the husband had been gifted £4.75 million for the purchase of the family home, with an additional sum of £500,000 for renovations. The husband received a further $8 million from his father, which was found to be a gift made for the husband's endeavours in the family business. The wife inherited £12 million from her late father (who died two years into the marriage). The husband sought to rely upon the pre-marital agreement, which elected a separation of property regime.

The court decided that the pre-nuptial agreement could be accorded no weight whatsoever. There were no previous discussions, the wife was young and had no knowledge or understanding of pre-nuptial agreements (although they were usual in the husband's family), the wife had no opportunity to seek legal advice and could not be said to have an appreciation of the terms or its implications. Furthermore, the wife was in a state of great turmoil, as her father had been diagnosed with a terminal illness in two weeks before signing the agreement.

The court found that the family home was part of the marital acquest, although tempered the equal sharing to reflect the origin of the asset. It would not have been fair to share the family home equally; however, it would not have been fair to exclude it entirely due to the length of the marriage and the fact that there were two minor children. Forty per cent

[90] *MT v VA (Second Application: Legal Services Provision Order)* [2020] EWHC 3087 at [84 – 85]

of the value of the family home was therefore treated as matrimonial and an additional sum attributable to the value of the husband's business interest was added, so that the family home was transferred to the wife outright and the husband retained his business assets.

***

It is clear from evolving case law that individual autonomy is being respected, post *Radmacher*. A nuptial agreement is likely to be upheld, providing the essential elements are present (and there are no vitiating factors).[91] Any award made contrary to the terms of a nuptial agreement is likely to be tempered only insofar as is required to ensure the parties' needs are met.

[91] See Chapter 4: Supreme Court

CHAPTER SEVEN

DRAFT NUPTIAL AGREEMENTS BILL

This chapter sets out the Law Commission's recommendations of 2014 and considers the Draft Nuptial Agreements Bill, which contains the recommendations.

The Law Commission Report

In 2009, the Law Commission began a project examining the enforceability and status of marital property agreements. This encompassed pre-nuptial agreements, post-nuptial agreements and separation agreements. The Law Commission received almost 150 consultation responses when its consultation was opened in January 2011, some of which resulted in the scope of the project being extended, in 2012, to include a targeted review of financial needs and non-matrimonial property.

The Law Commission's 'Matrimonial Property, Needs and Agreements Report'[1] ('the 2014 Report') was published on 27 February 2014, it having been extended in scope and in timeframe by 'significant events', namely the Supreme Court's decision in *Radmacher v Granatino*[2] in 2010 and the publishing of the Family Justice Review Final Report in 2011[3].

---

[1] The Law Commission's Matrimonial Property, Needs and Agreements Report 2014 can be found on the Law Commission website – https://www.lawcom.gov.uk/project/matrimonial-property-needs-and-agreements/

[2] *Radmacher v Granatino* [2010] UKSC 42

[3] D Norgrove, *Family Justice Review – Final Report (2011)*, as referenced in the Law Commission's 2014 Report

The 2014 Report primarily recommended:

(i) The law should be clarified in respect of the meaning of "financial needs", so as to ensure that there is consistency throughout the jurisdiction, by way of guidance published by the Family Justice Council.[4] The guidance should be addressed primarily to the courts but also be available, in plain English, to the public.[5] The guidance should be kept under review and updated regularly.[6]

(ii) There should be an investigation to assess whether or not any formulae could be devised that would be found useful in calculating "financial needs".[7]

(iii) Legislation should be enacted to introduce "qualifying nuptial agreements" that would be enforceable contracts and not subject to the court's overarching discretion, providing that certain procedural safeguards were met and the parties were not contracting out of "financial needs".

(iv) There should be a statutory abolition of the common law 'public policy' rule, that agreements made in contemplation of possible (rather than actual) separation are void.[8]

The Law Commission's recommendation to produce guidance on 'needs' has been actioned. The Family Justice Council has produced two guides: one for the public and litigants in person[9] and one aimed at the judiciary and legal advisers.[10] The practitioner's Guide is now in its second edition,

---

[4] The 2014 Report at [3.88]

[5] The 2014 Report at [3.89]

[6] The 2014 Report at [3.90]

[7] The 2014 Report at [3.159]

[8] The 2014 Report at [4.29] and [5.2]; note that the common law already recognises this, in *Radmacher v Granatino*

[9] The Family Justice Council – *Sorting out Finances on Divorce 2016 (April 2016)*

[10] The Family Justice Council – *Guidance on "Financial Needs" on Divorce, 1st Edition (June 2016)*

having been updated by a Working Group of experienced family finance experts, chaired by Mrs Justice Roberts in 2018.[11] Further guidance for the public has been produced by the charity AdviceNow.[12]

Qualifying Nuptial Agreements

The 2014 Report is often most renowned for its recommendation to introduce "qualifying nuptial agreements". The Report included a Draft Nuptial Agreements Bill, which is yet to be debated in Parliament. The Government's interim response came by way of two letters to the Law Commission, in April and September 2014. The Government considered there was insufficient time to debate the Bill before the dissolution of Parliament in March 2015 and, to date, the debate has not yet taken place. Government's final response is awaited.

In summary, the 2014 Report recommended:

- Qualifying nuptial agreements should be introduced by legislation.[13]
- Parties to an agreement would not be able to contract out of provision for financial needs.[14]
- Any dispute regarding a qualifying nuptial agreement should be heard by a family judge.[15]
- In an application for reasonable financial provision for a surviving spouse, under the Inheritance (Provision for Family and Dependants) Act 1975, the court should have regard to any

[11] The Family Justice Council – *Guidance on "Financial Needs" on Divorce, 2nd Edition (April 2018)*

[12] AdviceNow: *A Survival Guide to Sorting out your Finances when you get Divorced*

[13] The 2014 Report at [5.40]

[14] The 2014 Report at [5.84]

[15] The 2014 Report at [5.91]

provision in a qualifying nuptial agreement that relates to the claim.[16]

At Chapter 6 of the Report, the Law Commission recommended the following key requirements are met for a marital property agreement to be viewed as a qualifying nuptial agreement:

- The marital property agreement must be a valid contract.[17]
- A presumption of undue influence, which usually applies in contracts where there is a relationship of trust and confidence, will expressly not apply to qualifying nuptial agreements.[18]
- The marital property agreement must be made by deed.[19]
- The agreement should contain a clause, whereby the parties confirm they each understand the agreement is a qualifying nuptial agreement and that they are removing the court's discretion to make orders for financial provision, save for insofar as the agreement fails to account for needs.[20]
- Qualifying nuptial agreements would be invalid if made less than 28 days in advance of the marriage or civil partnership.[21]
- There should be disclosure, at the time of making the marital property agreement, of material information about the financial situation on both sides.[22]

---

[16] The 2014 Report at [5.124]

[17] The 2014 Report at [6.12]

[18] The 2014 Report at [6.29] (see below for further explanation)

[19] The 2014 Report at [6.36]

[20] The 2014 Report at [6.40]

[21] The 2014 Report at [6.67]; Note – the Law Commission makes no recommendation on timing in respect of post-nuptial agreements: [6.66]

[22] The 2014 Report at [6.91]

- Parties should not be able to waive their rights to disclosure.[23]
- Both parties must receive independent legal advice at the time the agreement is formed.[24]
- 'Legal advice' should include advice that: (i) the agreement is a qualifying nuptial agreement and the court will be prevented from making a different financial order, save so as to provide for financial needs; and (ii) the effect of the qualifying nuptial agreement on the rights of the party being advised.[25]
- A form of a statement of legal advice should be signed by both lawyer and client, which will create an evidential presumption that such legal advice has been given.[26]
- Any variation of a qualifying nuptial agreement must comply with all the pre-requisites for the formulation of a qualifying nuptial agreement[27] (save for the time factor, which is not a suggested requirement in respect of post-nuptial agreements).[28]
- A qualifying nuptial agreement may only be revoked by agreement, made in writing and signed by or on behalf of both parties.[29]

Two features of qualifying nuptial agreements warrant further explanation:

---

[23] The 2014 Report at [6.103]

[24] The 2014 Report at [6.125] and [6.159]

[25] The 2014 Report at [6.142]

[26] The 2014 Report at [6.145]

[27] The 2014 Report at [6.186]

[28] The 2014 Report at [6.66]

[29] The 2014 Report at [6.190]

Undue influence

The Law Commission recommended that the presumption of undue influence, which exists in contract law where there is a 'relationship of trust and confidence', should specifically not apply to qualifying nuptial agreements.[30] This is to mitigate a concern that a disproportionate number of financial settlements would likely be undermined due the risk of a presumption being found in every case.[31] Thus with the presumption removed, the burden of proving actual undue influence would continue to be on the party asserting it.

In considering the presumption of undue influence, the Law Commission made specific reference to the case of *NA v MA*,[32] which dealt with a post-nuptial agreement made after an adultery. It was found that the husband had exploited a dominant position in using the wife's adultery to induce her into entering the agreement. The agreement was found to have been made in circumstances such that it would have been unfair to hold the wife to its terms. Under the Law Commission's recommendations, a finding of undue influence would still make the contract voidable.

Revocation

Revocation occurs where both parties no longer wish to be bound by a nuptial agreement, but it would also be an appropriate step where there has been such a significant change in circumstances that variation is not suitable. The Law Commission is of the view that, given the contractual nature of qualifying nuptial agreements, it would be sensible to terminate the parties' obligations under any previous agreement by formally revoking it in writing.

---

[30] The 2014 Report at [6.29], [7.47]

[31] The 2014 Report at [6.28]

[32] *NA v MA* [2006] EWHC 2900

Impact of the Draft Bill

Qualifying nuptial agreements are not presently enshrined in law. The Nuptial Agreements Bill has not yet been debated in Parliament. Nuptial agreements are not presently binding and remain one of the circumstances of the case and subject to case law principles and the court's statutory discretionary exercise.[33] However, the position that has evolved, post-*Radmacher*, is not wholly dissimilar to that which is recommended by the Law Commission, albeit the framework lies under common law rather than a statutory one. Where there is a divergence in approach between case law and the Law Commission, the requirements of a qualifying nuptial agreement would be more robust (e.g. legal advice would be mandatory and parties could not opt out of receiving disclosure).

The Law Commission's recommendations are persuasive and have had an impact on general practice and the way in which nuptial agreements are drafted. Knowing that the recommendations may one day be implemented under statute helps practitioners to advise clients and prepare nuptial agreements in a way that is not contrary to the recommendations.

The introduction of a statutory framework could well crystallise the principle of autonomy in this jurisdiction. This could dramatically change the way in which financial provision cases are dealt with, particularly if an unforeseen consequence is a surge in separation agreements, where individuals are seeking to circumvent the court's discretion.

It remains to be seen, however, whether the introduction of a 'Nuptial Agreements Act' would make a difference in terms of post-separation litigation. The issues may well be narrowed, but if the Act provides (as recommended) that a qualifying nuptial agreement will be binding, save for where it does not provide for needs, the door will be left open

---

33 Section 25, Matrimonial Causes Act 1973 and Schedule 5, Part 5, Civil Partnership Act 2004

particularly where the agreement provides for needs and no more, due to the subjective nature of what constitutes 'needs'. Circumstances change, 'needs' change and it is likely that the most determined spouse or civil partner will not be discouraged from attempting to establish a greater 'need', whether through negotiations or via the court.

CHAPTER EIGHT

CREATING A 'FAIR' AGREEMENT

This chapter aims to identify the fundamental building blocks required to create a fair nuptial agreement.

Fairness: The Principle and the Test[1]

Fairness is the guiding principle in financial remedy cases. This is generally determined by the court checking its statutory discretionary exercise against the 'yardstick of equality'.[2] The court must make an order that is fair 'in all the circumstances of the case'.[3]

After ***White v White***[4], the House of Lords expanded further on the characterisation of fairness in the conjoined appeals of ***Miller v Miller and McFarlane v McFarlane***[5] and set out that 'fairness' is made up of three components: "…need (generously interpreted), compensation and sharing…"[6] The 'needs' principle is of elevated importance and practitioners will be aware that often the parties' needs (those for housing, income and retirement) dictate the outcome of financial remedy proceedings.

---

[1] Fairness, in general, and the principles underpinning it are considered in more detail in Chapter 2.

[2] *White v White* [2000] UKHL 54

[3] Section 25, MCA 1973

[4] *White v White, supra*

[5] *Miller; McFarlane* [2006] UKHL 24

[6] *Miller; McFarlane, supra, per* Lady Hale (then Baroness Hale of Richmond) at [144]

In ***Radmacher v Granatino***,[7] a three-stage fairness test was set out as applying to all nuptial agreements. In order for it to be fair to hold the parties to their agreement: (i) it must be freely entered into by both parties; (ii) they must have had a full appreciation of its terms and implications; and, (iii) in the circumstances prevailing at the time the financial order is being made, upon divorce or dissolution, it would be fair to hold the parties to the agreement. Once the court has decided the first two strands of the test are satisfied, it follows that there is a valid agreement and the court can then make an assessment in relation to the third.

Although a nuptial agreement can alter what would otherwise be deemed to be 'fair'[8], typically by contracting out of the sharing principle[9], it is clear from authorities that the statutory criteria[10] will remain at the forefront of the court's mind. Children must not be prejudiced by any nuptial agreement.[11] An agreement that fails to account for needs will be deemed unfair and is likely to be disregarded in part (and may well attract no weight at all).

Although a nuptial agreement is not legally binding, parties generally enter into one intending to be bound by its terms. As such, the presence of any standard vitiating factors (fraud, duress or misrepresentation) will negate the effect of an agreement and it will not be seen as enforceable. Such a finding would be contrary to the first part of the *Radmacher* Fairness Test[12] and it would not be considered fair to hold the parties to the terms.

---

[7] *Radmacher (formerly Granatino) v Granatino* [2010] UKSC 42

[8] *Radmacher v Granatino, supra,* at [75]

[9] *Brack v Brack* [2018] EWCA Civ 2862 at [106]; *Radmacher v Granatino, supra*

[10] Section 25, Matrimonial Causes Act 1973; Schedule 5 of the Civil Partnership Act 2005

[11] *Radmacher v Granatino, supra,* at [77]; *Luppi v Revesz* [2013] EWCA Civ 736

[12] *Radmacher v Granatino, supra,* at [75]

Both parties must have a full appreciation of the implications of the terms of the agreement. To ensure this is the case, it is desirable for both parties to receive independent legal advice. If legal advice is not obtained, this does not automatically invalidate the agreement. However, the absence of legal advice must be by choice and not because the party was prevented from obtaining it (including due to financial constraints). Full financial disclosure is ideal, but the onus is upon the other party to ask for it if disclosure is unsatisfactory (or, indeed, absent altogether). If a party is indifferent to detailed particulars of the other party's assets, this will not detract from the weight attributed to an agreement.[13] Adult autonomy reigns.

Once the first two elements of the *Radmacher* Fairness Test have been applied, the court will know whether or not there is a valid nuptial agreement. If the agreement has been fairly entered into and the parties are found to have had a full appreciation of the implications of the terms, it will naturally follow that a valid nuptial agreement was created. The court is then able to move on to the third strand: would it be fair to hold the parties to their agreement, in the circumstances prevailing at the time of making the order?[14]

The key consideration for the court, when determining whether to hold the parties to the valid agreement, is whether the terms of it create a fair result at the time they are seeking to implement the agreement. This requires application of the court's discretionary exercise and assessment of the three components of the fairness principle: namely needs, compensation and sharing. The existence of a nuptial agreement is likely to lead to a "modification of the sharing principle".[15]

The Law Commission stated in 2014 that, "The Supreme Court, in *Radmacher v Granatino*, has gone as far as it is possible for the courts to

---

[13] *Radmacher v Granatino, supra,* at [69]

[14] *Radmacher v Granatino, supra,* at [67]

[15] *Brack v Brack, supra,* at [88], quoting Lady Hale in *Radmacher v Granatino, supra,* at [177]

go in endorsing the validity of marital property agreements without an amendment of the statutory framework; only legislation can enable parties to enforce agreements without involving the courts' discretionary jurisdiction under the Matrimonial Causes Act 1973."[16]

The decision in *Radmacher* changes the landscape in respect of pre-nuptial agreements, but it can be seen that the courts had been building up to the changes for some years.[17] There had been a general (albeit slow in some quarters) shift away from the view that agreements made in contemplation of separation were 'void' for public policy reasons, into the realms of respect for parties' autonomy.

The safeguards that are required for an agreement to be valid, as identified in *Radmacher*, reduce – if not eradicate – the perceived vulnerability of a financially (and arguably emotionally) weaker spouse or civil partner. Most notably, they are that a party should not be prevented from obtaining independent legal advice and that the agreement is measured against a standard of fairness that ensures needs are met. Where two adults choose to enter an agreement between themselves, with a full appreciation of its implications, it is considered that it would be paternalistic and unfair not to hold them to their agreement.

Defining 'Fairness'

It is worth remembering that,

> **"…fairness, like beauty, lies in the eye of the beholder…"**[18]

As with all financial settlements, what constitutes a 'fair' agreement will depend on the circumstances of the particular case. It will be noted that

[16] The Law Commission Report 2014 at [1.34]

[17] See Chapter 3

[18] *White v White, supra, per* Lord Nicholls of Birkenhead, at [1]

the Court of Appeal (upheld by the Supreme Court), in *Radmacher*, considered it was fair for Nicolas Granatino to be allowed to keep the property acquired through the financial remedy proceedings only for so long as he would be required to maintain a home for himself and the two children of the family. The court gave a generous interpretation of the amount of time he would be required to keep and maintain a home for the children. He was allowed to retain properties in London (where he lives) and in the vicinity of the children's home with their mother until the youngest child is aged 22. The thinking behind this was so that Mr Granatino, who was described as 'extremely able'[19], would have had enough time until then to re-establish himself and achieve independence.

In light of this, it may be natural to assume that it would be sensible (at least for the party seeking to ringfence assets) to include such clauses in all nuptial agreements. It is, though, going to depend on the facts of the case being considered: it is highly unlikely to be fair to include such a reversionary interest in circumstances where the financially less-well-off party has a limited earning capacity or is the primary carer or homemaker.

At the beginning of the marriage between Katrin Radmacher and Nicolas Granatino, the husband was in a well-paid job and his earnings increased substantially during the initial years of marriage. Whilst he decided to change his career path during the marriage, the court considered it was fair to expect him to regain some, if not all, of his obvious earning capacity over the subsequent years. It is highly relevant that the husband sought a change in career for himself, rather than for the benefit of the family, which may otherwise have changed the degree of weight attributed to the nuptial agreement or provided him with the *prima facie* evidence to mount an argument for the court to apply the rarely invoked compensation principle.[20]

---

19 *Radmacher v Granatino, supra,* at [119]

20 See *SA v PA (Pre-marital agreement: Compensation)* [2014] EWHC 392 and *Waggott v Waggott* [2018] EWCA Civ 727

Not all cases will be suitable for a reversionary property interest and careful thought will be required as to whether or not this applies to an individual set of circumstances. In many cases it will be appropriate to simply meet the housing need of the less well-off party, without limiting the interest to a reversionary trust; however, this will be entirely fact-specific and the quest for fairness will need careful consideration.

Those signing any nuptial agreement must be alive to the fact that individual autonomy is very much respected; it is no longer considered to be contrary to public policy to hold parties to their pre-nuptial (or post-nuptial) agreement. If the less affluent party to a marriage chooses to accept the terms of a nuptial agreement, they are likely to be held to that agreement providing it meets their needs. A nuptial agreement is capable of altering fairness.[21] Therefore, even if the nuptial agreement includes terms that provide for an outcome that absent a nuptial agreement might not have been deemed to be the fair outcome, providing it meets needs, the parties are likely to be held to it. Caution is required.

The Magnetic Nature of Needs[22]

When a pre-nuptial or post-nuptial agreement is prepared, as with all financial remedy cases, the overriding relevant feature is that of 'needs'. It is suggested that, when drafting an agreement, careful thought ought to be given to whether a court would be satisfied that both parties' needs would be met and thus approve a consent order in the same terms, noting the existence of a nuptial agreement.

An agreement that fails to account for 'needs' is at high risk of not being upheld, in part or in whole. As stated by King LJ in ***Brack v Brack* [2018] EWCA 2862**, whilst fairness is likely to result in a court making a needs-

[21] *Radmacher, supra,* at [75]

[22] The court's treatment of needs is dealt with more fully in Chapter 2.

based award, the search for fairness may (albeit unusually) lead the court to make an award in excess of needs. [23]

There remains a degree of uncertainty in respect of nuptial agreements, as they are not binding and the court retains overall discretion as to the final order. The Supreme Court took the status of nuptial agreements as far as it could, in light of the statutory framework to which courts are obliged to consider.[24]

The Law Commission completed its report[25] on Matrimonial Property, Needs and Agreements in February 2014, a few years after the Supreme Court decision. It recommended that "qualifying nuptial agreements" be legislated for with strict conditions to be met before a marital agreement could become a contractually binding qualifying nuptial agreement, including that the agreement must not purport to exclude financial provision for needs.

In May 2016, a Private Member's Bill was presented to Parliament, to make provision for binding nuptial agreements subject to specified requirements, namely the Divorce (Financial Provision) Bill.[26] The Bill had its Second Reading in January 2017, but it did not progress further. The Government did not oppose the Second Reading but cited a concern that the proposed approach "…could cause hardship to many families; and that its proposals, which would radically change the law in this area, [had] not been subject to public consultation."[27]

During the Second Reading of the Private Member's Bill, the Government stated that the Law Commission's recommendations in respect of qualifying nuptial agreements would be considered "in due

---

[23] *Brack v Brack* [2018] EWCA 2862, *per* Lady Justice King at [103]

[24] Section 25 of the MCA

[25] The Law Commission Report is covered in more detail in Chapter 7.

[26] The Divorce (Financial Provision) Bill, presented by Baroness Deech

[27] House of Commons Briefing Paper 03752 on Pre-Nuptial Agreements, *per* Baroness Buscombe, responding on behalf of the Government

course in the context of [the Government's] wider plans for family law and system reform".[28] To date, there has been no further response to the Law Commission and the Draft Nuptial Agreements Bill has not been debated in Parliament.

[28] Baroness Buscombe, *supra*

CHAPTER NINE

DRAFTING AND REVIEW

This chapter is intended to provide practical guidance for those dealing with a nuptial agreement at the outset, whether instructed to draft, review or negotiate the agreement. It also explains the components that will attract or detract from the weight attributed to a nuptial agreement.

Key Ingredients and Features to Avoid

One of the primary aims of having a nuptial agreement is, usually, to avoid or limit post-separation litigation. The greater care taken when drafting an agreement, the greater chance there will be a better outcome for the parties, such that their divorce or dissolution will not result in a drawn-out, expensive and emotionally draining process.

A nuptial agreement is a bespoke marital contract, individual to the particular parties. It requires great thought and careful attention. There may be many hours of work involved, first through information gathering, then the drafting itself and, finally, negotiations. The terms of an agreement, the parties' property and their circumstances will differ in each case but the underlying principles and requirements for a valid nuptial agreement are the same. Creating an agreement that adheres to the features set out below will give the parties the best chance of creating an agreement that is upheld.

The agreement must not preclude the financial needs of either party and any children must not be prejudiced. Overall, for an agreement to be valid and endorsed in its entirety it must be fair (such that it would be unfair *not* to hold the parties to their agreement).

Aside from ensuring needs are provided for, noting that there is a degree of subjectivity as to what constitutes 'needs', there are some factors that must be avoided and some that must be included for the court to find that a valid nuptial agreement exists. Most factors are derived from case law. Others have evolved as best practice features, following the Law Commission's recommendations in 2014.[1] Some fall into both categories. Although the draft Nuptial Agreements Bill is yet to be debated in Parliament, it may be prudent for practitioners to adhere to the recommendations contained within the Bill.

Preparation

Invariably, the party wishing to ringfence property will lead the drafting process. That party will usually consult a lawyer to embark upon the preparation of the nuptial agreement. There would be a conflict of interest if a lawyer were to act for both parties and this would completely undermine any nuptial agreement made.

Before drafting an agreement, it is essential to hold a client conference, where the discretionary law of this jurisdiction can be explained, including the magnetic importance of 'needs'. Managing the client's expectations is key. The practitioner should also conduct a detailed fact-finding and information gathering session.

Disclosure

The Supreme Court has made it clear that a lack of disclosure will not, of itself, undermine an agreement. Instead, it is a 'material' lack of disclosure, information or advice that will weaken an agreement. The onus is on the other party to ask for disclosure; a clear indifference to disclosure will not diminish the weight attributed to a nuptial

[1] The Law Commission's Report on Matrimonial Property, Needs and Agreements Report 2014

agreement.[2] However, the Law Commission does recommend that parties should not be able to waive their rights to disclosure.[3]

Consideration ought to be given as to whether valuations are required. Arguably, if the principle is that a particular asset (e.g. a business) is ringfenced, the precise value is not necessarily 'material'; however, a significantly undervalued asset may prompt post-separation litigation.

Clients will need to understand that where values are provided, they should be authentic. If a client were to significantly downplay wealth, it might lead to the agreement not being upheld due to the other party not being appraised of the facts that would have been material to his or her decision or, possibly, an allegation of misrepresentation or fraud. Equally, if the financially weaker party were to present a more favourable financial position than reality, this could lead to a more limited assessment of needs.[4]

Full and frank disclosure is not necessary but there should be financial disclosure, so that the parties can be properly advised. A useful way to understand the asset base, and to ensure all assets are included, is to use Forms E as a basis for collating the information.

Schedules of Assets

It is advisable to create schedules of the parties' assets, liabilities and pensions, to be annexed to the deed of nuptial agreement. These do not have to be complicated, but the information will clearly show the financial positions of each party as at the date of the agreement. Schedules of assets will also provide a snapshot of any non-matrimonial, pre-acquired property, should it ever become an issue. It is therefore helpful to clearly label what the parties have agreed represents matrimonial and non-matrimonial property within the schedule.

---

[2] *Radmacher (formerly Granatino) v Granatino* [2010] UKSC 42 at [69]

[3] The Law Commission's 2014 Report, *supra*, at [6.103]

[4] *WW v HW (Pre-Nuptial Agreement: Needs: Conduct)* [2015] EWHC 1844

Deed

A nuptial agreement should be executed as a deed. This is recommended by the Law Commission[5] and will become law if the draft Nuptial Agreements Bill is passed. Best practice should be to create a deed, if for no other reason than to ensure that the legal status and implications of signing are fully appreciated.

Recording Background Circumstances

The mantra of anyone drafting a nuptial agreement ought to be, 'record, record, record!' Detail is everything when drafting a nuptial agreement. All circumstances and the parties' intentions should be recorded on the face of the deed. Arguably, this is particularly important for the person who wishes to protect property as there will be less opportunity, at separation, for the other party to claim circumstances existed that would undermine either the validity of or fairness of the nuptial agreement, should it later come to be relied upon.

Specifying all the circumstances pertaining to the creation of an agreement, and the parties' intentions at the time, will also assist the parties, lawyers and the court in understanding *why* the parties had made the agreement in the way they had, perhaps many years later. Notably, the recordings will demonstrate that each party received independent legal advice (or had the opportunity of doing so) on each aspect. Failing to record the circumstances and intentions may well result in costly post-separation litigation.

It will be noted that in several of the reported cases, the pre-marital agreements are said to be 'simple' documents, providing for a separation of property regime. The crucial feature is that such cases have involved pre-marital agreements created in another jurisdiction. In *Versteegh*[6], for example, the pre-marital agreement was stated to be a 'simple' agreement,

---

[5] The Law Commission's 2014 Report, *supra*, at [6.36]

[6] *Versteegh v Versteegh* [2018] EWCA Civ 1050

but pre-marital agreements are commonplace in Sweden and are generally enforced by the court. However, there is no requirement of an assessment of 'fairness' in Sweden. This naturally draws a distinction between the discretionary approach in England and Wales and in other jurisdictions.

It is prudent for those drafting pre-nuptial and post-nuptial agreements to record all relevant circumstances, on the face of the deed. These include (but are not limited to): the parties' age, background, whether they have been married or cohabited with anyone before; whether one party has paid for the other party's legal advice and that the other party has not sought to influence the legal adviser; whether a party has chosen not to obtain independent legal advice; whether the wedding or civil ceremony would go ahead without an agreement; defining the assets; if ringfencing is for inheritance planning, state why and who for; recording that the parties intend to create legal relations; the parties are satisfied they have all facts material to their decision to enter the agreement; they have a full appreciation of the terms and implications of the agreement and that they intend to be bound by them.

The Court's Discretion

It is important to remind clients that, just because the parties are agreed as to what will happen in the event of a relationship breakdown, it does not automatically follow that the court will do what they want the court to do. However, providing a valid nuptial agreement meets needs, and is fair, the court is likely to respect the parties' individual autonomy. Fairness, however, is a subjectively determined concept and will be assessed with the court having regard to all the circumstances of the case existing at the time of reliance upon it. The nuptial agreement will be just one factor to which the court must have regard, although it may be the most compelling factor in the case.[7]

[7] *Radmacher v Granatino, supra*

Practical Considerations

It is not uncommon for practitioners to be asked to draft a watertight agreement. As nuptial agreements are not contractually binding and the court retains overall discretion, it is not presently possible to achieve this; however, there are steps that may be taken to make it more likely that the agreement will be upheld.

The Supreme Court, in *Radmacher*, highlighted the components that would be required of a valid and fair nuptial agreement. These are considered in some detail in Chapter 4[8] and they should be given careful consideration whenever a nuptial agreement is being created or at any time one is the subject matter of legal advice.

Below are some practical points to bear in mind, which may assist when drafting or reviewing a nuptial agreement:

Identifying Needs

Parties to an agreement will be informed that a court is likely to respect their autonomous decision to enter into a pre-nuptial or post-nuptial agreement, providing that it is fair. It should be borne in mind that "…Fairness, like beauty, is in the eye of the beholder…".[9] However, it is likely to be unfair not to hold the parties to their agreement, providing that 'needs' are met.

'Needs' encompasses the parties' need for a home, income and during retirement. An agreement should ensure that both parties' needs are met and should not (in any circumstances) seek to exclude needs as this would create an inherently unfair agreement. A claim for spousal maintenance should not purport to be excluded.[10]

---

[8] Under the heading, 'The Supreme Court'

[9] *White v White* [2000] UKHL 54, *per* Lord Nicholls of Birkenhead

[10] *Hyman v Hyman* [1929] AC 601; *Z v Z (Financial Remedy: Marriage Contract)* [2011] EWHC 2878

It is up to the parties to negotiate for an outcome that is in their interests: the person seeking to ringfence assets is likely to want to limit the terms to the other party's needs but, as practitioners are aware, there are '*needs*' and '*needs*'. Negotiations may warrant recourse to the sharing principle (if bare needs does not already achieve an element of sharing), although there could simply be a generous interpretation of needs. It is a matter of negotiation as to how needs are construed and both parties must agree.

The parties' housing needs are of fundamental importance in terms of the capital distribution. It may be useful to define housing needs by identifying a property value and location that would adequately meet needs as at the time of making the nuptial agreement. If there are no children but they are contemplated in the immediately foreseeable future, it may be advantageous to identify two different scenarios of housing needs (i.e. what they would be with children and if the relationship remains childless). The housing needs could then be updated by reference to the Land Registry House Prices Index.

It may be appropriate to agree to transfer the family home into the parties' joint names, upon marriage, given the special status the family home has. However, practitioners acting for the party bringing the family home to the marriage will no doubt be mindful that with very high value properties, half of the value may exceed the other party's needs substantially. In such circumstances, it is likely to be enough to ensure that the housing needs of the other party will be met by distributing capital in an alternative way.

A party seeking to ringfence property may be reassured that if a review of the prevailing circumstances at the time of separation lead to a more generous offer of settlement than the strictly applied terms of a nuptial agreement would otherwise secure, the rest of the agreement will not be undermined.[11] However, it should be borne in mind that such a scenario may trigger at least some post-separation litigation.

---

[11] *Versteegh v Versteegh, supra*

If acting for the party who seeks to opt out of the sharing principle, it is likely that a generous interpretation of needs will be necessary and, depending on the asset base, even some sharing will be advised. However, often the party whose 'needs' are in question will say that they want to sign the agreement notwithstanding the advice to the contrary. Often the solicitor or barrister is presented with a pre-nuptial agreement and informed by the client that the terms have already been agreed. In circumstances where the client signs the agreement contrary to legal advice, it is imperative that the client signs a disclaimer setting out that they have chosen to enter a nuptial agreement despite being advised against it.

Those drafting an agreement should be mindful, when advising in respect of 'needs', of the extent to which the invasion of non-matrimonial property is necessary. If the parties are agreeing only to ringfence previously acquired property and intend for all future acquired property to be shared, the party without the ringfenced property may well have enough to be able to meet his or her needs without recourse to pre-acquired ringfenced assets; this will likely depend on the length of marriage and the extent of other assets.

In light of the *Radmacher* decision, the parties may well consider the grant of a reversionary property interest to last only whilst there are dependent children of the family. Caution should be exercised, however, as such an interest would likely create an unfair outcome unless the party benefitting from the property in his or her role as a parent has a good earning capacity or the ability to build up their own resources during that period of time. Although it may be appropriate to execute a charge where assets are more limited.[12]

Independent Legal Advice

Whilst case law does not regard independent legal advice as essential, the requirement is that both parties have a full appreciation of the terms and

[12] *V v V (Ancillary Relief: Pre-Nuptial Agreement)* [2011] EWHC 3230

implications of an agreement.[13] This becomes more of a challenge to prove where one party has not had the benefit of independent legal advice. The Law Commission's recommendations, for consideration by Parliament in the draft Nuptial Agreements Bill,[14] include a condition that independent legal advice would be crucial for any qualifying nuptial agreement.

Independent legal advice is desirable[15], as it protects both parties. For a party seeking to ringfence assets, it will provide assurance that the other party has been properly advised and does fully understand the terms and implications. If one party wants to opt out of the sharing principle, it will allow the other party to understand what would be given up and – if they still want to sign the agreement – negotiations conducted by their lawyer may lead to a greater share of the assets than otherwise would have been achieved.

A certificate of independent legal advice ought to be prepared, signed and appended to the nuptial agreement, if obtained, particularly for the benefit of a party seeking to ringfence assets. If one party is choosing not to obtain independent legal advice (from either a solicitor or a direct access barrister) and is therefore acting in person, the legal representative should ensure the litigant in person is reminded they should obtain independent legal advice and (as with all cases involving litigants in person) the legal representative should adhere to the 2015 guidance for lawyers[16], particularly with regard to communication and procedural assistance. If the litigant in person still chooses not to engage the assistance of an independent lawyer, it would be advisable to ensure this is recorded on the face of the nuptial agreement, together with a clause setting out that the party is satisfied they have a full appreciation of the

[13] *Radmacher v Granatino, supra*

[14] Considered in Chapter 7

[15] *Radmacher v Granatino, supra*

[16] Litigants in Person: Guidelines for Lawyers, June 2015 (produced by the Bar Council, CILEx and the Law Society)

terms of the agreement and its implications and is willing to be legally bound by them.

Practitioners should be mindful that if the reality is that the other party is not seeking independent legal advice because he or she lacks the financial means to do so, this is likely to fall foul of the Supreme Court's condition. The financially weaker party could mount an argument, at the time of reliance upon the nuptial agreement, that they were prevented from obtaining legal advice. This may lead to a finding that the agreement is unfair, as a party should not be disadvantaged by a lack of legal advice through a deficiency in resources.

In the situation of a party with limited assets, it would be appropriate for the financially stronger party to pay for the other party's independent legal advice; however, they should not (under any circumstances) seek to influence the choice of legal adviser, except to ensure that a specialist family finance lawyer is instructed. Directing the other party to a Resolution-certified solicitor,[17] is a good place to start. It is important to acquire expert review and advice from a family lawyer who specialises in financial remedies.

It is possible that the party seeking to opt-out of the sharing principle simply presents the lawyer with an agreement that he or she is willing to sign; however, this is not a tick box exercise. Full advice should be given. If the legal adviser considers it to be an agreement that should not be signed, but their client nonetheless wishes to proceed, it would be most prudent to obtain a signed disclaimer that the client has chosen not to accept the legal adviser's advice.

Where neither party has obtained legal advice, it is likely the court will respect parties' individual autonomy providing that each has understood the agreement's terms and implications and that the nuptial agreement meets needs. However, whether the nuptial agreement is upheld will

---

[17] Resolution Directory: resolution.org.uk

ultimately depend on the judge's assessment of all of the circumstances of the case.

Intention to create legal relations

The parties to an agreement, as autonomous adults, should intend the agreement to be binding upon them, notwithstanding that it is the court that will have the final say, and should intend that the terms of the agreement will be applied to their financial arrangements should there be a divorce or dissolution. Whilst the common law specifically does not require the parties to create a legally binding contract (because, by virtue of the Matrimonial Causes Act[18], the court retains its overall discretion),[19] such an intention does, nonetheless, demonstrate the parties' commitment to their agreement. Furthermore, the draft Nuptial Agreements Bill provides that the parties should intend to be contractually bound. Such an intention will ensure that parties' nuptial agreement complies with the Law Commission's recommendations, if the Bill is passed.

Often, pre-nuptial agreements have originated in other jurisdictions. Whilst a nuptial agreement created and signed in another jurisdiction does not add to the degree of weight attributed to it *per se*, it may, depending on the jurisdiction in question, go to the parties' level of understanding and awareness of the implications of the agreement. Particularly in jurisdictions where pre-nuptial agreements are commonplace and regarded as legally enforceable, it is likely the parties intended to be bound by the terms of the agreement.

Legal Professional Privilege

Lawyers should be mindful of privilege being waived inadvertently by a client. It should be remembered that the parties are likely to be on good terms at the time of drafting and they may be sharing information from

---

[18] Also the Civil Partnership Act 2005

[19] *Radmacher v Granatino, supra,* at [37]

their own lawyers. Always ensure when giving advice that the communications between a lawyer and their client are confidential, since they (invariably) will contain legal advice. The line of 'independence' may be crossed if the other side is influencing the instructions that are being provided.

Note that parties may well agree to waive legal professional privilege, should a dispute arise pertaining to the circumstances of signing the agreement. Good record keeping is essential, including recording any concerns about the client's demeanour, which may be relevant in terms of evidencing state of mind.[20]

Children

Children cannot be prejudiced by the terms of any nuptial agreement. The birth or adoption of children is a significant change in circumstances and fairness will likely dictate a higher assessment of needs. A short, childless marriage is clearly going to have a different level of 'need', particularly with regard to housing. Needs should be properly and carefully evaluated where there are children.

If children are contemplated and planned within the first few years of marriage, it would be useful to provide for this eventuality in the first instance, so that the parties are not forced to review and completely change their agreement in the first years of marriage. The agreement may record two housing needs, both with and without children. In either instance it may be useful to contemplate whether there is an expectation that the earning capacity and / or mortgage capacity of the party whose needs are in question would be maximised or, indeed, whether the property should be unencumbered.

It is good practice to record that where one party is wealthier, that party will ensure that any children of the family will be brought up in a lifestyle commensurate with his or her own. Precise child maintenance

[20] See *KA v MA (Pre-Nuptial Agreement – Needs)* [2018] EWHC 499

arrangements are unlikely to be included, as these will need to be assessed by reference to income, the child arrangements and possibly the standard of living at the time of separation. Any attempt to specify exact terms may inadvertently result in an agreement that is prejudicial to the children of the family.

Review

By their very nature, nuptial agreements cannot and should not be expected to cover every possible eventuality. There are innumerate unforeseeable situations that might arise creating a change in circumstances that would mean a nuptial agreement becomes inherently unfair. Review is not essential but the greater the passage of time between signing an agreement and reliance upon it, the more likely it is that circumstances will have changed and that parties will need to depart from its terms. It is therefore important to advise clients as to the need for review clauses and to provide for this within the agreement.

Whilst best efforts are made, there is an inherent difficulty in determining what a party's needs will be at an uncertain point in the future and so a provision for review at specified life events is useful to include within any pre-nuptial (or post-nuptial) agreement, together with a review at each 'x' number of years, in any event.

Parties may find that suggesting a review to their spouse is an area for controversy within the relationship and one party may refuse to engage with the review process. Since a review at life changes is not guaranteed, a further clause could be provided within the agreement to confirm that a failure to review will not undermine, invalidate or make void any other part of the agreement.

Undermining Factors

Practitioners need not be reminded that if any of the standard contractual vitiating factors (namely fraud, duress or misrepresentation) are present, the agreement will be attributed no weight at all. Undue pressure applied to one party would also be likely to eliminate the degree of weight attributed to an agreement; however, note that it is 'undue' pressure that will undermine an agreement, the sort of which would fall short of duress. Both parties may be under pressure of sorts, and this must not be mistaken for the sort of unconscionable conduct envisaged by the Supreme Court.[21]

Similarly, the exploitation of a dominant position in order to secure an unfair advantage would be viewed as unworthy conduct and the weight accorded to the nuptial agreement would either be reduced or eliminated altogether. Both parties must enter the agreement of their own free will.

Separation of Finances

Parties should ensure that if they have made a nuptial agreement ringfencing non-matrimonial property, they should continue to treat the said non-matrimonial property separately during the marriage. If they do not, then notwithstanding a court finding that a valid nuptial agreement exists, it may be deemed unfair to hold the parties to their agreement.[22]

Inheritance and Gifts

Inherited assets or gifts may form part of a nuptial agreement; if pre-acquired inherited or gifted property, a nuptial agreement will help to ensure they are ringfenced. If future inheritance is earmarked to be kept as separate property, often at the insistence of parents, it is worth advising the parents to take separate advice on wills, tax and inheritance generally; it may be appropriate to create a discretionary trust so as to protect those inherited or gifted assets further (noting the family court's discretion and subjective assessment of needs).

---

21 *Radmacher v Granatino, supra,* at [71]

22 *Currie v Monastyrski* [2017] EWCA Civ 1790

'Traditional' Relationships

Where the parties each assume 'traditional' roles of homemaker and breadwinner, it is unlikely to be considered fair for the homemaker to have opted out of all future marital acquest,[23] particularly given that the homemaker's contribution to the marital partnership will probably have enabled the breadwinner's career to flourish. In almost all cases, it is going to be likely to be fair to share property acquired during the marriage.

Limited Assets Cases

Case law naturally illustrates the treatment of nuptial agreements involving significant wealth; however, nuptial agreements certainly should not be seen as being applicable only in such cases. They are equally open to those who wish to ringfence pre-acquired property subject, of course, to the proviso that ringfencing will always be subject to needs.

The court's usual approach to non-matrimonial property (pre-acquired or inherited) may well result in property being ringfenced, with non-matrimonial property being invaded only to meet needs; however, post-separation litigation and arguments about the extent to which non-matrimonial property is to be ringfenced is likely to occur.[24] An agreement to ringfence only pre-acquired property or inherited property and to share all post-acquired property, depending on the circumstances of the case, has a greater chance of being upheld where the other assets are sufficient to meet needs.

In cases with limited assets, recording a mutual intention to ringfence pre-acquired or inherited assets is of elevated importance to seek to avoid expensive post-separation litigation that the parties can ill afford. However, where assets are more limited, it may not be reasonable – or possible – to ringfence a pre-acquired asset, particularly where the asset in question becomes the marital home. Nonetheless, a short, childless

---

[23] *Radmacher v Granatino, supra,* at [81]

[24] See Chapter 2 for further detail

marriage or civil partnership is more likely to enable an element of ringfencing, providing that both parties can meet their needs.

Time Limits

In 2014, the Law Commission recommended that qualifying nuptial agreements should be introduced by legislation. One of the recommendations was that such agreements should be invalid if made less than 28 days before the date of marriage or civil partnership. Although the Nuptial Agreements Bill has remained in draft form, it has nonetheless become general best practice to ensure that a pre-nuptial agreement is executed by the parties no less than 28 days before the 'Big Day'. Whilst the Law Commission's recommendations are no doubt influential and should continue to be adhered to wherever possible, case law does not presently support the contention that an agreement signed less than 28 days in advance will automatically invalidate the agreement.

In fact, the contrary is true. Many agreements signed less than 28 days beforehand have been upheld by the court. Whether or not a failure to adhere to the time limit will be fatal to the validity of an agreement will depend on the circumstances pertaining to the late signing. The key factor for the court to consider is not *when* the agreement was signed but whether or not the party seeking to depart from the agreement had a full appreciation of the terms and implications of it.[25]

The late signing of a pre-nuptial agreement would not, of itself, amount to a finding of undue pressure. There may well be time pressures but undue pressure requires there to have been unconscionable conduct, which falls short of duress.[26]

In ***K v K***,[27] the wife signed the agreement three days before the marriage and she was held to its terms, having fully understood the agreement and

---

[25] *Radmacher v Granatino, supra*

[26] *Radmacher v Granatino, supra,* at [71]

[27] *K v K* [2003] 1 FLR 120

having been properly advised as to its terms at the time. Notably, it was found that she was not under undue pressure, she exercised her own free will and the husband had not exploited a dominant position. Further, although there was no full disclosure this was not deemed to be a factor that would undermine the agreement because the wife did not ask for it. Importantly, there were no unforeseen circumstances. Although this case was decided pre-*Radmacher* the principles applied accord with the Supreme Court's decision.

In ***Versteegh***,[28] the pre-nuptial agreement was signed one day before the wedding and was upheld; however, this was a very simple document and commonplace in Sweden, where the parties (who were Swedish nationals) married. It is also of note that the court accepted the husband's evidence that they had discussed and agreed the terms months in advance.

The High Court, in ***SA v PA***,[29] found a pre-nuptial agreement to be valid even though it was signed only on the eve of the wedding ceremony. Although this was short notice, the court was satisfied that the wife had a full appreciation of the agreement's terms and implications. Notably, the agreement was made in respect of surplus property only (i.e. it did not purport to exclude needs) and it did not attempt to exclude spousal maintenance.[30]

Despite these decisions, it is better to ensure an agreement is signed at least 28 days before the wedding or civil ceremony. This will no doubt go a considerable way to avoiding any arguments that the lateness of signing the agreement meant that there was not enough time to reflect and properly consider its terms. If an agreement is signed very close to the wedding but there have been ongoing negotiations for some time in the lead-up to the signing, any argument as to lateness will be

[28] *Versteegh v Versteegh* [2018] EWCA Civ 1050

[29] *SA v PA (Premarital Agreement: Compensation)* [2014] EWHC 392

[30] *Hyman v Hyman* [1929] AC 601; *Z v Z (Financial Remedy: Marriage Contract)* [2011] EWHC 2878

significantly weakened. However, since the purpose of entering into an agreement is ultimately – at least in most cases – to limit (or perhaps eradicate) post-separation litigation, it would be more advantageous to settle a pre-nuptial agreement well in advance of the marriage or civil partnership.

It is not uncommon to be approached to draft a pre-nuptial agreement in the final weeks of wedding preparation. The first advice to a party seeking to ringfence pre-acquired wealth ought to be to consider postponing the wedding to allow more time for the agreement to be properly considered and drafted. This may cause difficulty and friction between the parties but in order to ensure that an agreement is not undermined by time pressures, this is probably the best option.

Arguably, the second-best alternative is to create a post-nuptial agreement in mirror terms to the pre-nuptial agreement, to be signed shortly after the date of marriage or civil partnership. The court no longer draws a distinction between pre-nuptial and post-nuptial agreements, but the post-nuptial agreement will serve to demonstrate that the parties had time for reflection, were not under any pre-wedding pressure and they nonetheless confirmed their intentions. This approach is not without its challenges (as one party may refuse to sign) but it would be a way of confirming their autonomous choice, absent any apparent time pressures.

Jurisdiction

Parties should identify their choice of jurisdiction, which will regularly be 'England and Wales'. It is useful to record that the parties understand their agreement is not presently automatically binding in this jurisdiction, despite their intention to be bound by its terms.

Parties may wish to elect a different jurisdiction to have the final say over any disputes relating to their financial settlement. Any prorogation clause should be clear and should not require complex drafting.[31] A client

[31] *Brack v Brack* [2018] EWHC 3431

should obtain the advice of a lawyer in the elected jurisdiction to understand the implications of electing the alternative jurisdiction and should understand that the discretionary approach afforded in this jurisdiction will not apply if the prorogation clause is found to be valid and their case is determined in the elected jurisdiction.

Confidentiality

Nuptial agreements and the parties' financial arrangements is often a sensitive topic for discussion and the parties may choose to be bound by a confidentiality clause. In some cases, such as where there are famous parties or commercially sensitive business assets confidentiality clauses will be essential.

Data Protection (GDPR)

As a subscript, it is worth noting the GDPR rules. For practitioners responsible for drafting a nuptial agreement, GDPR rules should be considered for two reasons: firstly, the legal adviser's usual privacy policy may need to be amended so as to include a nuptial agreement specific clause; and, secondly, so that a client's consent to contact for any review of the agreement is obtained.

It is usual practice to retain papers for seven years; however, it may well be appropriate to retain files for longer, for example seven years after the financial settlement on divorce or death of either party (whichever is the earlier). It would generally be regarded as best practice to either obtain a client's specific consent or simply make it part of a privacy policy.

Practitioners may wish to obtain consent to contact the client in advance of the set time of review, although it should be made clear that the onus is on the client to review (so as not to inadvertently lay oneself open to a possible claim if contact is not made).

CHAPTER TEN

ADVISING AT SEPARATION

This chapter aims to set out the key considerations for those instructed to deal with a divorce or dissolution where a nuptial agreement exists, whether acting for the party who seeks to rely upon the agreement or acting for a party seeking to undermine it.

Initial Consultation

A party seeking advice in respect of their divorce or dissolution may refer to the existence of a nuptial agreement. The advising lawyer may either be faced with a party who intends to be fully bound by the agreement, or one who may regret signing the agreement and wishes to go behind its terms. Naturally, the legal adviser will request a copy of the agreement and advise accordingly.[1]

The agreement should be carefully read and the circumstances pertaining to the creation of the agreement, alongside the prevailing situation should be fully understood. The client ought to be reminded of this jurisdiction's status as a discretionary system but also that the agreement is likely to be upheld, providing that it is fair and meets the needs of the parties. It is worth spending time to consider whether the agreement properly meets both parties' needs, and all of the factors set out by the Supreme Court should be taken into account.[2]

[1] See Chapter 9 for practical considerations

[2] See Chapter 4: 'The Supreme Court'

Enforcing an Agreement

All of the *Radmacher*[3] features (and those in subsequent case law) ought to be considered whenever faced with a nuptial agreement at separation. Where a party is seeking to rely on a nuptial agreement, particular thought ought to be given to the following: whether the parties have kept their finances separate, if as planned[4]; whether there is a change in circumstances such that would change the basis of the agreement; whether the agreement meets the needs of both parties (and any children, if applicable); and whether the agreement was entered into pre-*Radmacher* (and whether this has an impact in terms of the legal advice received).

If a client fairly recognises that the nuptial agreement falls far short of meeting the other party's needs, he or she may consider making an offer to the other party that is more generous than that set out in the agreement. This will not negate the general terms of the agreement.[5]

Notice to Show Cause

A party seeking to rely upon the terms of a nuptial agreement may do so by issuing a notice to show cause as to why the other party considers that an order in excess of that provided for by the nuptial agreement should be made. This may be issued as a freestanding application[6], as it is not necessary for there to be existing proceedings, although the procedure to be followed will likely differ depending on whether financial proceedings have been initiated. The Family Procedure Rules 2010 do not stipulate a particular process for notice to show cause applications.

---

[3] *Radmacher (formerly Granatino) v Granatino* [2010] UKSC 42

[4] *See Currie v Monastyrski* [2017] EWCA Civ 1790

[5] *Versteegh v Versteegh* [2018] EWCA Civ 1050

[6] *Hopkins v Hopkins* [2015] EWHC 812; *KA v MA (Pre-nuptial Agreement: Needs)* [2018] EWHC 499

If a Form A[7] has been issued, the proportionate approach would be to agree directions, in respect of the notice to show cause application, either at the first appointment or via submitting agreed directions to the court, vacating the first appointment until there has been a determination of the notice to show cause proceedings. If there is no Form A, the application for notice to show cause ought to be made using Form D11 and the Part 18 (FPR 2010) procedure followed.

Whilst a notice to show cause application may be detached from financial proceedings, it will be necessary for the court to understand the asset base. Making such an application in respect of a pre-nuptial or post-nuptial agreement is quite distinct from an application made in respect of a *Rose* agreement[8], made after a financial dispute resolution hearing, or even a *Xydhias* agreement[9], where heads of agreement have been reached. In either case, the agreement is based on presently prevailing financial circumstances, the parties' disclosure duties will have been invoked and the court appraised of the parties' present financial situations.

The court must have all relevant information and may wish to make directions with regard to evidence, being mindful of the overriding objective and proportionality. Where a notice to show cause application has been made, supporting documentation with Forms E are unlikely to be required unless the court determines the nuptial agreement to be invalid or inherently unfair.

The court is likely to require witness statements, detailing the parties' respective positions in respect of the circumstances attending to the formation of the nuptial agreement, so that the application is not considered "...in a vacuum with no consideration of the surrounding circumstances of s25 factors..."[10] However, in a case with facts as

[7] The form issued to begin financial proceedings on divorce or dissolution

[8] *Rose v Rose* [2002] EWCA Civ 208

[9] *Xydhias v Xydhias* [1998] EWCA Civ 1966

[10] *S v S* [2008] EWHC 2038, *per* Eleanor King LJ at [23]

exceptional as in ***Crossley v Crossley***[11], where the pre-nuptial agreement was "...a factor of magnetic importance..." it is likely to be in the interests of justice to preclude further disclosure and adopt an abbreviated procedure to determine the financial application, on application of the court's discretionary exercise.

Challenging an Agreement

The paradigm shift in the way nuptial agreements are regarded by the court, post *Radmacher*, means that parties must be very careful about opting out of the sharing principle. The court's respect for an individual's autonomous right to decide how they would like to treat their finances arising from a marriage or civil partnership reigns, and the court's search for fairness will usually lead to a court upholding the terms of a valid nuptial agreement, providing that it meets needs.

When seeking to challenge an agreement, attention should first be paid to its inception. The background circumstances are highly relevant (hence why it is useful to record all background circumstances existing at the time on the face of the deed of pre-nuptial or post-nuptial agreement).

There is a hierarchy of possible grounds[12] that may undermine an agreement. Firstly, there are factors that would challenge the validity of the agreement altogether; secondly, there are elements that would make the agreement inherently unfair; thirdly, where the nuptial agreement fails to provide for the needs of the spouse seeking to go behind the agreement, such that it produces an unfair result at the time of separation.

The key question ought to be whether there is evidence of any of the standard vitiating factors, which would (if proven) eliminate the weight

[11] *Crossley v Crossley* [2007] EWCA Civ 1491, involving a short, childless marriage, a pre-nuptial agreement and both parties brought substantial wealth to the marriage

[12] See Chapter 4: *'The Supreme Court'* for the full list of features which may add to or detract from the weight attributed to a nuptial agreement

attributed to the nuptial agreement altogether. It is likely that cogent independent evidence will be required to establish a claim of fraud, misrepresentation or duress. The existence of any of the vitiating factors will negate the agreement altogether.

If unconscionable conduct (like undue pressure which falls short of duress) can be proved, the agreement is likely to be attributed no weight. If there is evidence of unworthy conduct, such as exploitation of a dominant position to secure an unfair advantage, the weight attributed to the agreement is likely to be reduced or even eradicated.

Careful consideration of the background circumstances, in an early client conference, may lead to a conclusion that there may be grounds to challenge the inherent fairness of an agreement, including (but not limited to):

- time and other pressures (such as emotional, impending wedding, possibly a pregnancy. However, it is important to remember that both parties may have been under the same pressures and it is the full appreciation of terms that matters);
- no independent legal advice (and the client had been prevented from obtaining it);
- material non-disclosure (and the client had requested it);
- ringfenced post-acquired wealth, in a 'traditional' relationship (i.e. where one party is the breadwinner and the other cares for the home and family).

If the legal adviser instructed to consider the nuptial agreement at the time of separation was not involved in the drafting process, the previous solicitors' file is very likely to be of assistance.

After establishing the circumstances existing at the time the agreement was made, contemplation of the prevailing circumstances must be considered, notably: whether there has been a change in circumstances, including the arrival of non-contemplated children; whether the agreement meets the needs of the client (for a home, income and during retirement). The client's needs should be identified and if the circumstances demand an increase in the division, an offer should be formulated for consideration by the other party. The parties may agree to engage in alternative dispute resolution, such as mediation or arbitration. However, if negotiations are unsuccessful to the effect that the other party refuses to vary the agreement insofar as meeting needs, court proceedings may need to be issued. A notice to show cause application may follow and so the client may wish to issue Form A, to at least ensure that the timetable is implemented and Forms E (likely without enclosures)[13] can be completed.

It is worth noting that a change of circumstances could affect the fairness of the agreement on both sides. Practitioners should also be mindful to consider whether there has been a change of circumstances that have had a significant detrimental impact on the 'wealthier' party's needs, particularly with regard to earning capacity. If the 'wealthier' party has suffered a change, such as ill-health, a disability or failed business, it may not be fair to hold the parties to their agreement and the assets may need to be split in a different way, perhaps on a needs basis on both sides. Of course, a nuptial agreement is just one of the section 25 factors; the parties' health and earning capacities may become very relevant and the degree of weight attributed to an agreement could diminish.

Ultimately, if the pre-nuptial or post-nuptial agreement is well-drafted and considers all the appropriate factors, then realistic advice needs to be provided to the client. It is unlikely to be in the client's interests to expend on legal costs to challenge a well-drafted and properly considered nuptial agreement. That said, if 'needs' are not properly met, or the agreement is otherwise unfair, it may be worth challenging.

Given the discretionary nature of the court system, a judge's determination of 'needs' may be at a level higher than otherwise provided for within the agreement. Negotiations, therefore, might achieve a better

---

[13] *Crossley, supra*

outcome for the client and the other party might be willing to increase the capital, income or pension provision, so as to avoid facing costly and risky litigation. However, as with all family finance cases, the costs / risk benefit of ongoing litigation (on both sides) must always be weighed in the balance.

MORE BOOKS BY LAW BRIEF PUBLISHING

A selection of our other titles available now:-

'A Practical Guide to Solicitor and Client Costs – 2nd Edition' by Robin Dunne
'Constructive Dismissal – Practice Pointers and Principles' by Benjimin Burgher
'A Practical Guide to Religion and Belief Discrimination Claims in the Workplace' by Kashif Ali
'A Practical Guide to the Law of Medical Treatment Decisions' by Ben Troke
'Fundamental Dishonesty and QOCS in Personal Injury Proceedings: Law and Practice' by Jake Rowley
'A Practical Guide to the Law in Relation to School Exclusions' by Charlotte Hadfield & Alice de Coverley
'A Practical Guide to Divorce for the Silver Separators' by Karin Walker
'The Right to be Forgotten – The Law and Practical Issues' by Melissa Stock
'A Practical Guide to Planning Law and Rights of Way in National Parks, the Broads and AONBs' by James Maurici QC, James Neill et al
'A Practical Guide to Election Law' by Tom Tabori
'A Practical Guide to the Law in Relation to Surrogacy' by Andrew Powell
'A Practical Guide to Claims Arising from Fatal Accidents – 2nd Edition' by James Patience
'A Practical Guide to the Ownership of Employee Inventions – From Entitlement to Compensation' by James Tumbridge & Ashley Roughton
'A Practical Guide to Asbestos Claims' by Jonathan Owen & Gareth McAloon
'A Practical Guide to Stamp Duty Land Tax in England and Northern Ireland' by Suzanne O'Hara
'A Practical Guide to the Law of Farming Partnerships' by Philip Whitcomb

'Covid-19, Homeworking and the Law – The Essential Guide to Employment and GDPR Issues' by Forbes Solicitors

'Covid-19, Force Majeure and Frustration of Contracts – The Essential Guide' by Keith Markham

'Covid-19 and Criminal Law – The Essential Guide' by Ramya Nagesh

'Covid-19 and Family Law in England and Wales – The Essential Guide' by Safda Mahmood

'A Practical Guide to the Law of Unlawful Eviction and Harassment – 2nd Edition' by Stephanie Lovegrove

'Covid-19, Residential Property, Equity Release and Enfranchisement – The Essential Guide' by Paul Sams and Louise Uphill

'Covid-19, Brexit and the Law of Commercial Leases – The Essential Guide' by Mark Shelton

'A Practical Guide to Costs in Personal Injury Claims – 2nd Edition' by Matthew Hoe

'A Practical Guide to the General Data Protection Regulation (GDPR) – 2nd Edition' by Keith Markham

'Ellis on Credit Hire – Sixth Edition' by Aidan Ellis & Tim Kevan

'A Practical Guide to Working with Litigants in Person and McKenzie Friends in Family Cases' by Stuart Barlow

'Protecting Unregistered Brands: A Practical Guide to the Law of Passing Off' by Lorna Brazell

'A Practical Guide to Secondary Liability and Joint Enterprise Post-Jogee' by Joanne Cecil & James Mehigan

'A Practical Guide to the Pre-Action RTA Claims Protocol for Personal Injury Lawyers' by Antonia Ford

'A Practical Guide to Neighbour Disputes and the Law' by Alexander Walsh

'A Practical Guide to Forfeiture of Leases' by Mark Shelton

'A Practical Guide to Coercive Control for Legal Practitioners and Victims' by Rachel Horman

'A Practical Guide to Rights Over Airspace and Subsoil' by Daniel Gatty

'Tackling Disclosure in the Criminal Courts – A Practitioner's Guide'
by Narita Bahra QC & Don Ramble

'A Practical Guide to the Law of Driverless Cars – Second Edition'
by Alex Glassbrook, Emma Northey & Scarlett Milligan

'A Practical Guide to TOLATA Claims' by Greg Williams

'Artificial Intelligence – The Practical Legal Issues' by John Buyers

'A Practical Guide to the Law of Prescription in Scotland' by Andrew Foyle

'A Practical Guide to the Construction and Rectification of Wills and Trust Instruments' by Edward Hewitt

'A Practical Guide to the Law of Bullying and Harassment in the Workplace'
by Philip Hyland

'How to Be a Freelance Solicitor: A Practical Guide to the SRA-Regulated Freelance Solicitor Model' by Paul Bennett

'A Practical Guide to Prison Injury Claims' by Malcolm Johnson

'A Practical Guide to the Small Claims Track' by Dominic Bright

'A Practical Guide to Advising Clients at the Police Station'
by Colin Stephen McKeown-Beaumont

'A Practical Guide to Antisocial Behaviour Injunctions' by Iain Wightwick

'Practical Mediation: A Guide for Mediators, Advocates, Advisers, Lawyers, and Students in Civil, Commercial, Business, Property, Workplace, and Employment Cases' by Jonathan Dingle with John Sephton

'The Mini-Pupillage Workbook' by David Boyle

'A Practical Guide to Crofting Law' by Brian Inkster

'A Practical Guide to Spousal Maintenance' by Liz Cowell

'A Practical Guide to the Law of Domain Names and Cybersquatting'
by Andrew Clemson

'A Practical Guide to the Law of Gender Pay Gap Reporting' by Harini Iyengar

'A Practical Guide to the Rights of Grandparents in Children Proceedings' by Stuart Barlow
'NHS Whistleblowing and the Law' by Joseph England
'Employment Law and the Gig Economy' by Nigel Mackay & Annie Powell
'A Practical Guide to Noise Induced Hearing Loss (NIHL) Claims' by Andrew Mckie, Ian Skeate, Gareth McAloon
'An Introduction to Beauty Negligence Claims – A Practical Guide for the Personal Injury Practitioner' by Greg Almond
'Intercompany Agreements for Transfer Pricing Compliance' by Paul Sutton
'Zen and the Art of Mediation' by Martin Plowman
'A Practical Guide to the SRA Principles, Individual and Law Firm Codes of Conduct 2019 – What Every Law Firm Needs to Know' by Paul Bennett
'A Practical Guide to Adoption for Family Lawyers' by Graham Pegg
'A Practical Guide to Industrial Disease Claims' by Andrew Mckie & Ian Skeate
'A Practical Guide to Redundancy' by Philip Hyland
'A Practical Guide to Vicarious Liability' by Mariel Irvine
'A Practical Guide to Applications for Landlord's Consent and Variation of Leases' by Mark Shelton
'A Practical Guide to Relief from Sanctions Post-Mitchell and Denton' by Peter Causton
'A Practical Guide to Equity Release for Advisors' by Paul Sams
'A Practical Guide to the Law Relating to Food' by Ian Thomas
'A Practical Guide to Financial Services Claims' by Chris Hegarty
'The Law of Houses in Multiple Occupation: A Practical Guide to HMO Proceedings' by Julian Hunt
'A Practical Guide to Unlawful Eviction and Harassment' by Stephanie Lovegrove
'Occupiers, Highways and Defective Premises Claims: A Practical Guide Post-Jackson – 2nd Edition' by Andrew Mckie

'A Practical Guide to Financial Ombudsman Service Claims' by Adam Temple & Robert Scrivenor
'A Practical Guide to Advising Schools on Employment Law' by Jonathan Holden
'A Practical Guide to Running Housing Disrepair and Cavity Wall Claims: 2nd Edition' by Andrew Mckie & Ian Skeate
'A Practical Guide to Holiday Sickness Claims – 2nd Edition' by Andrew Mckie & Ian Skeate
'Arguments and Tactics for Personal Injury and Clinical Negligence Claims' by Dorian Williams
'A Practical Guide to Drone Law' by Rufus Ballaster, Andrew Firman, Eleanor Clot
'A Practical Guide to Compliance for Personal Injury Firms Working With Claims Management Companies' by Paul Bennett
'A Practical Guide to Dog Law for Owners and Others' by Andrea Pitt
'RTA Allegations of Fraud in a Post-Jackson Era: The Handbook – 2nd Edition' by Andrew Mckie
'RTA Personal Injury Claims: A Practical Guide Post-Jackson' by Andrew Mckie
'On Experts: CPR35 for Lawyers and Experts' by David Boyle
'An Introduction to Personal Injury Law' by David Boyle
'A Practical Guide to Subtle Brain Injury Claims' by Pankaj Madan

These books and more are available to order online direct from the publisher at www.lawbriefpublishing.com, where you can also read free sample chapters. For any queries, contact us on 0844 587 2383 or mail@lawbriefpublishing.com.

Our books are also usually in stock at www.amazon.co.uk with free next day delivery for Prime members, and at good legal bookshops such as Wildy & Sons.

We are regularly launching new books in our series of practical day-to-day practitioners' guides. Visit our website and join our free newsletter to be kept informed and to receive special offers, free chapters, etc.

You can also follow us on Twitter at www.twitter.com/lawbriefpub.

www.ingramcontent.com/pod-product-compliance
Lightning Source LLC
LaVergne TN
LVHW022047200926
848481LV00003B/817